Talking About
Being Your Best

More Books from A GIRL'S WORLD:

Talking About Friends

Talking About Boys

Talking About Growing Up

Talking About Family

Talking About My Life

A Girl's World Presents

Talking About
BEING YOUR BEST

Real-Life Advice from Girls Like You

Created by A Girl's World Productions, Inc.
and the members of www.agirlsworld.com

Edited by Sara Sauceda
With Lynn Barker and Karen Willson

PRIMA PUBLISHING

Copyright © 2001 by A Girl's World Productions, Inc.

All rights reserved. No part of this book may be reproduced or transmitted in any form or by any means, electronic or mechanical, including photocopying, recording, or by any information storage or retrieval system, without written permission from Random House, Inc., except for the inclusion of brief quotations in a review.

Published by Prima Publishing, Roseville, California. Member of the Crown Publishing Group, a division of Random House, Inc.

PRIMA PUBLISHING and colophon are trademarks of Random House, Inc., registered with the United States Patent and Trademark Office.

All of the characters in this book are based on real persons, but in some cases, names have been omitted or changed to protect the privacy of the people involved. Therefore, any resemblance to actual persons, living or dead, is purely coincidental, unless authorized by the actual person mentioned.

Library of Congress Cataloging-in-Publication Data on File
ISBN 0-7615-3295-1

01 02 03 04 05 HH 10 9 8 7 6 5 4 3 2 1
Printed in the United States of America

First Edition

Visit us online at www.primapublishing.com

First, with grateful hearts we dedicate this book to God, who in 1996 gave us the idea to go out and build a place on the Internet where what girls think, feel, and do really does matter.

We dedicate this book to the millions of girls who have used their time and talent to share their thoughts, hopes, and dreams with all the other girls of the world at www.agirlsworld.com.

With love and peace, we dedicate this book to all of our volunteer girl editors (past and present), our AGW Girlcrew, our adult volunteers, advisors, webmaster, families, and friends who've worked so hard to make A Girl's World a reality.

Contents

Preface xi
About A Girl's World: What Makes This Book Special xiii
Introduction: Share the Dream xv

CHAPTER 1: BECOMING THE BEST STUDENT YOU CAN BE 1
What's the Best Way to Improve Study Habits? 1
How Can I Take the Best Class Notes Ever? 3
What's the Best Way to Find Time to Study? 5
What's the Best Way to Stop Procrastination? 10
What's the Best Way to Study Math? 15
What's the Best Way to Study History? 17
What's the Best Way to Keep from
   Freezing Up on Tests? 23

CHAPTER 2: DOING YOUR BEST IN SCHOOL ACTIVITIES 27
What's the Best Way to Run for
   School Office and Win? 27
What's the Best Way to Get a Part
   in the School Play? 33
What's the Best Way to Start a Club
   and Keep It Running? 37
What's the Best Way to Get "In" and
   Hang with the Hotties? 40

What's the Best Way to Prepare for an
Audition for Band or Chair Test?................... 41
What's the Best Way to Get Noticed at School? 43
What's the Best Way to Deal with a
Pep Squad Tryout?.............................. 46

CHAPTER 3: DEVELOPING YOUR BEST MIND 51
What's the Best Way to Learn a New Language? 51
What's the Best Way to Improve Bad Spelling? 55
What's the Best Way to Learn Science?................ 60
What's the Best Way to Memorize
Dialogue in a Play?............................. 64
What's the Best Way to Tune Up Your Imagination? 65
What's the Best Way to Tune Up
Your Sensory Perception? 67
What's the Best Way to Tune Up Your Self-Esteem? 68
What's the Best Way to Get Over Writer's Block? 68
What's the Best Way to Remember Everything?......... 71
What's the Best Way to Memorize Music? 78

**CHAPTER 4: LOOKING AND
FEELING YOUR VERY BEST..................... 81**
What's the Best Way to Feel Good About Your Body? 81
What's the Best Way to Tune Up Your Body? 83
What's the Best Way to Deal with Acne? 86
What's the Best Way to Stop Having Bad Hair Days? 89
What's the Best Way to Deal with Sweat?.............. 91
What's the Best Way to Live and Be Totally Fit? 93
What Are the Ten Best Ways to Feel Good Inside? 97
What's the Best Way to Learn About Fashion Fast? 101
What's the Best Way to Try Modeling?................ 103

CHAPTER 5: PERFORMING YOUR BEST IN SPORTS ... 105

What's the Best Way to Pick a Sport to Play? 105
What's the Best Way to Deal with Refs? 106
What's the Best Way to Deal When
   You're No Good at Sports? 107
What's the Best Way to Fit into a Team? 111
How Can I Play My Best Game on
   an All-Boys Team? 112
What's the Best Way to Boost My Skills? 114
What's the Best Way to Deal When You
   Don't Make the Team? 115
What's the Best Way to Begin Track? 116
How Do You Get the Best Out of
   Your Sports Tryout? 117
What It Was Like: Trying Out for Basketball 118
What It Was Like: Trying Out for Football. 119
Specific Sports Tips 119

CHAPTER 6: BEING YOUR BEST AT HOME 123

Vacation Time Is Boring! What's the
   Best Way to Have More Fun? 123
What's the Best Way to Share a Room? 126
What's the Best Way to Borrow or Lend Money? 132
What's the Best Way to Deal When
   Your Brother Is Autistic? 135
What's the Best Way to Deal When Siblings Tease? 137
What's the Best Way to Deal When Friends
   Make Fun of Your Mom? 141
What's the Best Way to Buy a Gift for Your Guy? 143
What's the Best Way to Get and
   Keep Your First Job? 146
What's the Best Way to Throw a Party? 151

CHAPTER 7: BEING THE BEST PERSON YOU CAN BE 153
  What's the Best Way to Start at a New School? 153
  What's the Best Way to Be Both Smart and Cool? 155
  What's the Best Way to Deal with Being Bullied? 157
  What's the Best Way to Tame a
    Maxed-Out Schedule? 168
  What's the Best Way to Deal with Stress? 172
  What's the Best Way to Stop Being Too Emotional? 179
  I Love Animals! What's the Best Way
    I Can Help Them? 182

CHAPTER 8: BEING YOUR BEST AT WHATEVER YOU DO 187
  What's the Best Way to Start a Band? 187
  What's the Best Way to Get into a
    Chorus or Choir? 189
  What's the Best Way to Make a Student Video? 195

CHAPTER 9: JOIN THE FUN! 199
  What People Are Saying About Us 199
  What Girls Say About AGW 201
  What Adults Say About AGW 202
  Awards 203
  Use the Gold Key Chat Club to Meet New Friends! 203
  Problems? Get Help! 204
  Membership Form 205

Meet the Editor 207

Preface

Hello, I'm Sara Sauceda. I have been a member (on and off) of A Girls' World since 1996. The club is a place where girls can give advice to each other, write their own books, and have total GIRL POWER. Many girls go to AGW for help when they are confused, scared, or sad, and many come to have fun and enjoy themselves.

Girls all around the globe visit AGW on the Web and submit advice questions to be answered. Our volunteer columnists write an answer and send it back to the club to be published weekly. If you are on the Web, here is where you can find advice: www.agirlsworld.com/info/advice.html.

We got the idea to publish this book when we realized that not every girl has the Internet. We want every girl to get advice from real girls and teens. My favorite thing about these books is that they are helping girls all over the world, and I am very proud to be a part of it all. AGW also features fun and entertaining articles written and edited by girls all over the world. Whatever brings you and your friends to www.agirlsworld.com, there is always something or someone that will be there for every girl.

The purpose of this book is to help girls get through the tough and confusing times in their lives and discover how to be the very best at almost everything that's important to girls. Not only will this book answer many of your questions, but it's also a whole lot of fun. There are interesting quizzes, quotes, Talk Abouts for you and your friends, WebWatch's to go exploring, fun stuff to do, and places where you can journal and doodle. Enjoy your book, have lots of fun, and remember, Girls Rule!

If you have any questions or comments about this book, e-mail me by visiting www.agirlsworld.com. I'd really love hearing from you. My penpal number is 210893. I hope you enjoy *Talking About Being Your Best* as much as I enjoyed editing it.

Sincerely,

Sara Sauceda
Girl Editor, A Girl's World Online Clubhouse

About A Girl's World: What Makes This Book Special

"Help me! I'm desperate!" When searching for the "how-to's" of growing up, pre-teen and teen girls most appreciate advice from their peers. Whatever life throws at a girl, however embarrassing or challenging, another girl has been through it and can help. If trying to be the best "you" possible is over-the-top on your stress meter, then *Talking About Being Your Best* is here to help. Getting real-life advice for girls, by girls is what this book is all about. And what better advice is there than reading about another girl who has "been there and done that"?

The material in this book was written, edited, and/or suggested by girls and teens from around the world. Girls ask the questions, and other girls—not grownups—answer them. As members of the adult "Girl's World" team, we had the opportunity to help collect, shape, and do a final edit on this book. But what you're holding is truly girl-powered, and that's what makes it special. It is important to our Girlcrew that readers are able to react to what they read here. That's why we hope you enjoy the many opportunities to journal, doodle, talk to your friends, and turn this book into a one-of-a-kind treasure chest you've created that will contain your blueprint for building the best girl possible: YOU!

Lynn Barker and Karen Willson
Adult Editors, A Girl's World Online Clubhouse

Introduction: Sharing the Dream

Everything in this book and on www.agirlsworld.com was thought up, planned out, written, and/or edited by girls and teens the world over. Our mission is to create a space in the world that is entirely girl-powered. We're all about what's possible in a bright future created by girls and teens.

After you've read this book, you're invited to get in on the fun. Do you have any stories or advice you'd like to contribute? Your thoughts and opinions about this book really matter to us. Here's how to get in touch or send us submissions for the next book on how to deal with your life.

Submissions online:
www.agirlsworld.com/clubgirl/scoop/index.html

Comments online:
www.agirlsworld.com/best.html

Submissions or comments by email:
editor@agirlsworld.com

Subject line:
Talk About: Being Your Best

Mailing Address:
A Girl's World Productions, Inc.
ATTN: Talking About Books Editor
825 College Blvd.
PBO 102-442
Oceanside, CA 92057
(760) 414-1092 messages

Becoming the Best Student You Can Be

What's the Best Way to Improve Study Habits?

The Problem Dear Being Your Best: I would like it if you would tell me how to study for tests and how to understand homework. I have a really big problem with study habits and homework! If you could help me, I would greatly appreciate it.

—Jen, 14, Pennsylvania

A Solution I am really glad I get to answer your question! I am 17 and about to enter my final year, so I have had lots of practice at studying. I find that throughout high school, students are told to study and do homework but are not taught how this should be done. So I will share my study techniques with you.

Tests usually make up a large portion of your final grade, so it is important that you do well on them. Because you have

NEED HOMEWORK HELP?

The Homework Help site has lots of links to other sites that can answer questions or help you out.

www.albedo.net/~arvic/homework.html

to learn a month or more worth of work, just studying the night before is not enough! This is called cramming, and it does *not* work! You should study even when you don't have tests! I study most nights. This is not as bad as it sounds. I have an exercise book for each subject, and when I get home from school, I summarize what I have learned in my lesson in dot points (using examples when they are needed). Maybe one sentence on each point. This only takes me 5 or 10 minutes, and sometimes I don't do any at all because the ideas have already been covered.

On the weekend I spend up to 30 minutes reviewing what I have learned for that week and testing myself. If I have a test coming up, I will spend about 10 to 15 minutes each night leading up to the test studying. I find that if you study for tests throughout the school year, you don't have to spend much time studying when it is time for final tests or exams.

Highlighters are great inventions (and not just for decorating your page!). When I get a homework assignment, I highlight the due date, form (essay, report, multiple-choice questions, short-answer questions, etc.), and the main ideas (what the final product should say). If you understand the question and don't leave parts out, you will get higher marks. If the mark scheme is recorded on the assignment sheet, be sure you read it. Are there points for presentation, grammar, spelling, fluency, or extra information? Remember to check your homework twice; check it in your head and then leave it for a while. When you go back to it, read it out loud. This is helpful because when you start spending a lot of time on an assignment, you start seeing it as you would like it to be—not as it is. Once you understand what it is you're supposed to be doing, it's much easier to get it done! Don't forget to ask questions if you don't understand; that's what teachers are for!

Time management is also important in study. Homework is not always fun, and when you have lots of other things to do, it is easy to blame not having enough time. I make a plan so that I can find time for all the things I want to do. This is how I make mine: I get a piece of plain paper and divide it into seven columns and mark the first five into half-hour blocks from the time school starts until bedtime. I then divide the Saturday and Sunday columns into smaller hour sections. Then I record all my commitments (except study and homework). Then I put in my study time. I don't fill my homework in because the amount of time I have to spend on each subject varies, but the planner lets me see how much spare time I have. My planner also shows me when I should say NO to extra commitments. This is especially helpful at exam time.

Hopefully now you can study well. It may seem like a lot of work, but it's not as much as it can be if you try to do all your work at the last minute. Studying is not hard work, but it must be regular. Don't worry—you'll be a pro in no time!

—Sonya, 17, Australia

How Can I Take the Best Class Notes Ever?

What to Write Down

- The teacher will usually announce the topic for that class. Write the topic down. If she or he doesn't mention the topic, ask.

- If the teacher writes something on the board, write it down in your notes.

What to Listen and Look For
- Important dates
- Key people
- Names of places
- Key concepts
- Words your teacher defines on the board
- Any kind of math or science formula

How to Make Your Notes Work for You
- Get a study partner who takes notes in class.
- Compare your notes with a classmate's. See if you missed anything.
- Go over your notes as soon as you can after class.
- Never copy notes over again. Make notes on your notes instead.
- If you have time between classes, scan your class notes and use a highlighter to get the four main points.
- Be sure to review your notes before the next day. Just read them over.
- Is there something you're totally clueless about? Write down your question and ask the teacher first thing the next day or before class.
- Go to your teacher during office hours for help, too.

How to Study at Home
- Try to remember what the teacher's main point was for that day. Put that point on the top of your note page for the day.

- Circle the four most important points the teacher tried to cover.
- Put a check mark in the margin next to important ideas.
- Put more than one check mark if it's *really* important.
- Once a week, make a summary sheet of the points you circled or checked.

Remember that school is for a good reason. With it, you can be a SUCCESS!!! Just remember that, and it will keep you determined to do your best. I'm sure all of us care about our future!

— Umbro, an AGW member

What's the Best Way to Find Time to Study?

The Problem Dear Being Your Best: I'm in Scouts, sports, and drama. It's really hard to find time to study. What do I do?

— Veronica, 12, California

A Solution Dear Veronica: Managing time is an important skill that you can learn. Giving yourself the gift of regular, scheduled time to study is probably one of the biggest keys to success in school. We asked some A students how they managed to find the time. Here are their tips.

What You'll Need to Manage Time
- a nice, quiet place all to yourself (if possible) where you can do homework
- a pencil or pen

- a date book or calendar
- a school scheduler
- an open mind

Step One: Keep Track of Your Time
- Get a scheduler.
- Mark in your classes.
- Mark in your sleep time.
- Mark in your travel time to and from school.
- Write in appointments you can't get out of, such as doctor visits and allergy shots.

Step Two: Set Priorities
- Set goals for yourself at the beginning of every week.
- Prioritize tasks you need to do. What tasks do you need to accomplish? Which ones are most important? That's your priority for the week.
- Start with the most important task that you have to finish.
- If a task is important, do it now. Don't put it off.
- Split the big jobs up into smaller pieces. Does a project look too big to do? Divide it into parts that are easy to finish.

Step Three: Schedule According to Your Priorities
- You should plan on at least 2 hours a week of study time for every class you have. How many classes do you have? If you have six classes, that means 12 hours of study time, 2 hours a day, six days a week. Plan on more time if a subject is hard for you. Figure at least 2 hours of study a day for six days.
- Next, schedule in your activities: band practice, sports, ASB, science club, scouts. Put in times you've said you'd do something, like sports practice or an after-school job.

- If you find you don't have time to sleep or call your friends, you are doing too much! Cut back, but not on your study time. Decide that study has to come first.

- If you have busy parents, schedule days during the week when you can, for example, go to the library for a project, and tell them in advance when you need to go. Writing your parents a note can often help, especially if they're the forgetful kind and you need supplies for a project.

- Write down all your assignments on a calendar or in a little pocketbook. That way you won't forget them.

- Try to get together with your friends a couple times a month, and plan your time according to your homework/extracurricular activity schedule.

Do not dwell in the past, do not dream of the future, concentrate the mind on the present moment.
—Buddha
Submitted by
Shantelle, 13, USA

Step Four: Maximize Your Time

- Figure out when you're most alert—during the morning, afternoon, or evening. Study when you are most alert. Some kids study best before breakfast, or after dinner. It's different for everyone.

- Make study dates with yourself and keep them.

- You'll do better if you study the same subject at the same time and day of the week. It's weird, but your body learns better when it knows what to expect.

Q. I think my best friend might be jealous. I started getting all A's in school, and, well, she's not. Now she seems cold toward me. Do you have any advice?

—Amanda, 11, California

1 I would see what subjects she needs help in and offer to study with her to help bring up her grades.
Mostly disagree   Somewhat disagree   Somewhat agree   (Mostly agree)

2 Try to get her talking about stuff other than school. Get her mind off grades and on interests that you both share.
(Mostly disagree)   Somewhat disagree   Somewhat agree   Mostly agree

3 I'd just ask her if she feels bad because you are suddenly making better grades. Tell her that shouldn't make any difference in your friendship.
Mostly disagree   Somewhat disagree   Somewhat agree   (Mostly agree)

4 Just set up some study dates with her. While you are studying, answer any questions she might have on the work. In other words, help her improve her grades without letting her know you are doing it.
Mostly disagree   Somewhat disagree   Somewhat agree   (Mostly agree)

5 If people don't like you because you make better grades, then they aren't real friends. I'd dump her.
(Mostly disagree)   Somewhat disagree   Somewhat agree   Mostly agree

- Don't have homework? Do a weekly review of your notes. It'll really pay off when you're getting ready for exams.

Step Five: Manage Your Study Time
- Study your hardest subject first. That way you won't be tired and you'll learn more.
- Study your easiest subjects last.
- Don't cram or study more than a few hours. It doesn't work.
- Set an alarm clock and take a break every hour.
- When your brain hits overload, switch subjects.
- Don't study math, then science right after. Change subjects. Like do math, then art or English or history. Why? You'll use different parts of your brain.
- Study in the same place. Not your bed or the kitchen table. Use a desk, away from the TV or radio.

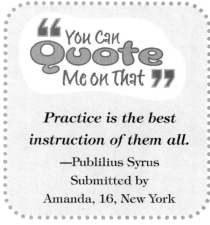

Practice is the best instruction of them all.
—Publilius Syrus
Submitted by
Amanda, 16, New York

- Emergencies will happen and eat up your study time. Stop and immediately plan when you'll make up the time you missed.
- Sundays are a great make-up day.
- Don't forget to study between class time. Even 15 minutes is great. Don't always wait for a 2-hour block of time.

Step Six: Dealing with Time-Stealing Emergencies
- Plan for interruptions. They'll happen!
- Don't flip-flop your decisions. Make up your mind and go with it. Don't dither.

- Spend your energy focusing on the job at hand.
- Plan how to do what you are doing before you begin.
- Finish what you start before starting something else.
- Learn to say yes to yourself and no to others. There's not much more important than learning.
- Don't read junk mail.
- Try to do more than one chore (or all your chores) at one time.
- Don't try to do things perfectly. Try to do them well.
- Don't try to do everything for everybody. Don't over-schedule yourself.

—Nicole, 15; Eva, 13; Brittany, 16; Michelle, 14; and Carolyn, 16

What's the Best Way to Stop Procrastination?

First, you have to know when you're procrastinating. You know you're procrastinating (putting off starting things) when you say, "Hey, I work better under pressure" or "Don't worry, I'll do it later" or "I don't feel like it."

Recognize any of these lines?

> She gives too much homework. It's her fault I can't get it all done.
> I'll start it tomorrow.

But I don't know where to start!
I've got to give myself a break.
Things aren't that bad.
I've got lots of time to get things going.
I've got too much to do first. I'll get to it!

If any of these sound familiar, you're probably procrastinating. Here are some ways to break that habit.

How to Stop Procrastination

- When you hear yourself say, "Hey, I work better under pressure," say "No you don't!" Then *do* it!

- When you hear yourself say, "I'll do it later," do it *now*. You'll feel better after it's done and have more time to do other things.

- When you hear yourself say, "I don't feel like it," remind yourself that your feelings don't rule your life! Besides, you'll feel better knowing the work is out of the way so you can play! When you hear yourself say, "She gives too much homework. It's her fault I can't get it all done," decide maybe your teacher is trying to challenge you to grow your mind. Do *more*. Do *your best*. Rise to the challenge!

STUDY SMARTER

Here's a Web site that might help with your homework. Try Homework Central by Big Chalk.com

www.bigchalk.com

- When you hear yourself say, "I'll start it tomorrow," start it today. You'll feel great! And starting is the hardest part of any task.

Talk About

Q. For some reason I just can't seem to get into studying for my big tests. It seems impossible, and I can't seem to study because I don't know where to begin. What would you do?

— Andrea, 11, California

1 I'd just make sure I was in a quiet place with no distractions. Just put all your concentration on your books.

Mostly disagree   Somewhat disagree   Somewhat agree   Mostly agree

2 I'd team up with a fellow student who makes good grades and has good study habits. Ask if you can study with this person for the test. Then make sure you stick to studying.

Mostly disagree   Somewhat disagree   Somewhat agree   Mostly agree

3 I'd talk to my teacher about my study problems. What does she or he suggest to help me concentrate on studying for the test?

Mostly disagree   Somewhat disagree   Somewhat agree   Mostly agree

4 I would go through all the material that might be on the test, underline the most important facts, make a list, and start memorizing.

Mostly disagree   Somewhat disagree   Somewhat agree   Mostly agree

5 I'd ask my parents to get me a tutor to help me concentrate and figure out a method of study that works for me. Everyone has a method that works best for her or him.

Mostly disagree   Somewhat disagree   Somewhat agree   Mostly agree

- When you hear yourself say, "But I don't know where to start," ask your friend for advice. When you hear yourself say, "I've got to give myself a break," work for an hour, then take a break. You'll have really *earned* it!

- When you hear yourself say, "Things aren't that bad," realize that they will get worse if you don't get things done that are important to you.

- When you hear yourself say, "I've got lots of time to get things going," challenge this idea. You'll have *more time* to yourself if you get your work out of the way.

- When you hear yourself say, "I've got too much to do first. I'll get to it!", look at your goal and priority list. Figure out whether this task you are avoiding is a priority or not.

> **" You Can Quote Me On That "**
>
> *The roots of education are bitter, but the fruit is sweet.*
>
> —Aristotle
> Submitted by
> Samantha, 17, Florida

Get Yourself Moving! Motivation

- Remember why you're in school. To earn money as a grownup, you have to learn. Knowledge is earning power!

- Flex those "finish it!" muscles. The more you finish on time, the easier it will be next time.

- Toss the words "should," "could," "would" from your thinking. Replace them with "can," "will," "want to." You don't know what you can do until you try your hardest.

- Say yes to success.

- Find things that stretch your idea of what you can do.

- Imagine yourself achieving your wildest dreams. Take the chance of finishing things!

- Don't avoid problems. Solve them! Practice making good decisions.

- Find out what you're good at. Do that!

Tips for Getting Things Done

- If you have a lot of homework, break it up.

- If you know the math paper will be a cinch, do it *after* the hard English assignment. This will give you a break from all the hard work.

- The big science test is coming up, along with the easy social studies quiz. Try some science and then have a small snack, like an apple. Come back and try more science.

- If you plan to study for an hour, study for a half-hour, then take a short break for 5 minutes. Walk around your backyard, draw a picture in the other room, something relaxing away from your study area. Reading some other tough book will just give you more stress.

- And the number one thing NOT to do while studying is to study science then take a "break" by studying social studies! This will mix you up, and you might say the organ that works the least on a 24-hour basis is South America. Mixing subjects while studying is not good. (Mixing homework is okay, but not studying.)

- Try studying in a different order than your classes. By January, always doing science, then reading, English, history, and math will get boring and may make you not pay attention. Try math first, followed by a little English for a change!

—Article by Meg K., 12, Australia

What's the Best Way to Study Math?

What do the A students know that most kids don't? We asked A students to tell us their secrets at being their very best at math! Here's what a few of them say:

Learning math is exactly like learning a sport. Math has nothing to do with smarts and everything to do with regular practice. Here are some tips to help you out.

Before Class

- Schedule time to look over yesterday's class notes every day, before your next class. Keep what you learned in the last class fresh in your mind.

In Class

- Write down any concepts your teacher puts on the board. You'll need to know these for the test!

- Stop at a new concept. Write it down. Puzzle it out.

- If you get lost, don't wait. Immediately ask your teacher for help!

- Make notes on any new concepts and formulas you just learned.

START A MATH-BUSTERS STUDY GROUP

Put together a study group. Make friends with people who seem to really like math. Get together once a week for a math-pizza party. Make everyone in the study group do a problem. Cheer them on! (No slackers!) Do the problems together, and then reward yourself with a pizza party!

Don't forget to tell your teacher about your group. Ask for extra problems for your study group to do. Your teacher won't forget you when grade time comes around!

- Don't be surprised if you don't get a new concept after two or three readings. Hey, it's new!

MAKING MATH FUN!

Make a game show out of your math problems! Here's how:

- Get a blackboard. (Use an empty classroom if possible.)
- Divide up into two teams.
- Have each team pick a problem and challenge the other group to work it.
- Be sure each group explains how they worked it.
- The team that answers the most questions right wins!

At Home

- Do the homework, even if you don't have to turn it in.
- Read your math book very carefully. Don't try speed reading or skimming.
- If your teacher gives you problems to solve, look back over your notes.
- Ask yourself: Which concepts, rules, or formulas were covered in class? Will any of them help solve this problem?
- Make up your own practice tests from your notes.

I remember in 7th grade, my pre-algebra teacher was TERRIBLE. He didn't teach very well at all. Most of the parents complained, but that doesn't really help the F's you get on quizzes. The best thing to do then is just take the book home and teach yourself. I know it sounds like a pain, but it was either that or summer school.

— Liz R., USA

To be successful in math: Always check your work.

— Laura H., USA

What's the Best Way to Study History?

What do the A students know that most kids don't? We asked A students to tell us their secrets at being their very best at history! Here's what a few of them say:

I like history because you learn how to be a detective. By looking to see why people did things, you find out why things are the way they are. It makes me wonder what will happen next.

—Lauren B., 8th grade

The Scene of the Crime . . . Reading Right

- Look at the overview and index first. After that, read the introduction.

- Every history book has a point to make. The introduction has clues about what the point is.

- Pretend your history book is like a mystery novel. Who are the main characters in this week's chapter? What do they want? Why do they want it? Who stands against them? What do the heroes have to change to get what they want? Do they get it? What stops them?

- Have a pen and paper handy, and get ready to survey your reading.

Bored by the Past? Try This!

People who lived long ago were a lot like the kids in your class. Some of them wanted to change their world for the better. Some wanted to keep everything the way it was. Others just wanted to have a place to live, food to eat, and a good time. When you look back into the past, ask yourself these questions:

What was life like for a kid my age?
What problems did they want to solve?
Were there homeless people? A drug problem? Did people make laws to try to control teen behavior?
How did kids get together to goof off?
How did kids rebel?

Pick a problem or a topic, such as teens and the law. Find out all you can about that problem or topic. Read books. Go online. Find out what solutions the people long ago tried. Did their solutions work? Find out who the heroes, heroines, and bad guys were. How did they spread the word or communicate without TV or radio? What plans did they make? How did they make things happen? What did they do to hang in there when things went wrong?

Step One: Find the Clues When You Read

- Scan. Glance over the whole chapter. Read it, but read it fast.

- Ask yourself: Why did the writer write this? What is this chapter about?

- Don't worry about little facts. Get the big idea first.

- Is the writer for something? Against it? What's his or her complaint?

- If you see something you don't get, like a new word, put a check mark in the margin next to it.

- Don't stop reading.

- Whatever you do, keep reading all the way to the end.

- Now pretend you're answering this question: What's the point? What happened here that is important? Why is it important? All writing starts with a main idea. What's the writer trying to say? Write down the writer's main point on your paper. Don't go on until you get what they were trying to say. Still don't get it? Look at the first sentence of every paragraph for clues. *Hint:* A writer often makes a statement, then uses the rest of the chapter to prove the point.

• Still lost? Look at the headline or title of the chapter. That may help.

• If you can't find it, ask for help. Ask how that person knew what the main point of this chapter was about. Make them show you by pointing out the clues.

Step Two: Catch What You Missed

• Go back to your check marks.

• Look up any words you didn't know in a dictionary.

• Write down what they mean.

• Now go back and re-read those sentences. Do they make more sense?

MAKE HISTORY COME ALIVE!

Here are some fun things to do together with friends to make history come alive!

• Watch a video together that covers the time you are studying.

• Try a recipe from that period, or do a craft from that time. There are books in the library with recipes and ideas about what to do.

• Make history come alive by acting out a play; re-create a historical scene you just read about.

• Borrow (age-appropriate) historical fiction from the library. There are romances and detective fiction and diaries from many time periods.

• Get some of those cool history kits with fun projects: making papyrus, excavating a dig, or putting together a 3-D castle jigsaw puzzle. Ask an adult to supervise, and then try making the craft from the kit.

Step Three: Be a Detective

• Read through the chapter slowly.

• Can you spot the introduction? That's the place where the writer first makes the point about what happened that was important. Circle the introduction with a pencil.

• Check the next couple of paragraphs. Look for what facts the writer gives out to prove the point. Circle those facts.

• Next, look at the last paragraph. Lots of times, writers make their point again and sum it all up at the end. Check to see if this is the same point you wrote down on your paper. If you got the point the first time, that's great! If you wrote down something very different, make changes to what you wrote, or rethink your idea of what it's about.

Step Four: Make a Decision

• Now ask yourself: Why did the writer write this article? Do you agree with what the writer said? Or do you disagree?

• Writing is a lot like an argument. The writer is trying to prove something with facts. Did they prove anything to you? What facts made you agree or disagree with the writer's point?

• Here are some specific suggestions:

Before Class Starts

• Scan over what you read the day before.

• Look ahead at the chapter that is next. Get an idea of what the new topic is.

• If your teacher hands out a syllabus (class schedule), glance at it to see where this info fits in.

• Daydream for a moment. Do you already know something about this topic? What do you know?

- Look at the chapter headings, charts, and pictures. Get a picture in your mind of what the new chapter is all about.

- Write down any terms you don't understand. Find out their definitions. Or ask the teacher if you don't understand something.

- Pay close attention to anything in **bold** or *italics*. The author is trying to get your attention!

- Dig through the diagrams and charts. Try to get what point they are making. Don't skip any diagrams, charts, or illustrations. They usually point out important facts, events, or historical figures you'll need. To remember more, close your eyes and see if you can picture the chart in your mind. That will help you remember the information.

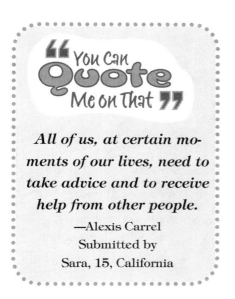

All of us, at certain moments of our lives, need to take advice and to receive help from other people.

—Alexis Carrel
Submitted by
Sara, 15, California

In Class

- Write down any facts, dates, or ideas your teacher puts on the board. You'll need to know these for the test!

- If your teacher gives you essay questions to think about, try them out. To find the answers, look back over your notes.

- Ask yourself: Which historical figures or ideas, dates, or events were covered in class? Will any of them help me write this essay?

- Make up your own practice tests from your notes.

- If you get lost, don't wait. Immediately ask your teacher for help!

And another strategy:

History Homework Help

- Schedule time to look over your class notes every day.
- Make notes on any new events, facts, historical figures, or information you just learned.
- Read over any new chapters or material.
- Plan to take a 10-minute break for every hour of study.
- Stop if you feel overwhelmed. Give yourself time.
- Getting lost or bored? Talk to yourself! No kidding . . . stop at the end of each paragraph to say out loud what it was about.
- Use your reading to fill in any important facts missing from your class notes.
- Don't highlight or underline bunches of text. Not everything is of major importance.
- Redraw the diagrams and charts yourself. That helps you remember them.
- Stop and review your class notes at least once a week.

FUNfest

MAKE YOUR OWN EGYPTIAN CARTOUCHE

A cartouche is your official Egyptian nameplate. Make one for yourself or a friend. Cool!

www.seaworld.org/Egypt/cartouche.html

Start a History Study Group

- Put together a study group. Make friends with people who seem to really like history. Then get together once a week.

- Go over your notes as a group.

- Make flashcards and play games to remember key historical figures and facts.

- Do your homework together. Be sure everyone in the study group has a turn at the flashcards or answers a homework question. Then reward yourself with a pizza party!

- Don't forget to tell your teacher about your group. Ask for extra homework or reading or ideas on how you can make history come alive in your study group. Your teacher won't forget you when grade time comes around!

- If in the end you just don't understand, don't be afraid to ask questions. There is no such thing as a wrong or right question.

—Amanda O., 11, Minnesota

What's the Best Way to Keep from Freezing Up on Tests?

The Problem Dear Being Your Best: Please help! I'm having a problem with English class. I always seem to freeze up when I have a project due or if I have to write something in class, especially something timed. This has happened for a long time (since about third grade), and I don't know what to do about it. The thing is, I don't have any problem with spelling, grammar, or anything else; it's just that my mind always seems to go blank. If you have any advice, I would be grateful.

—Student, 13, Ohio

A Solution

Hey, Student! Well, as you probably know, this problem is due to nervousness or worry. You know that you are good at English, but when there is pressure on you, you suddenly go blank. This is a common problem, but that doesn't make it any easier!

What you have to do is this:

- *Take a deep breath* and tell yourself that this one exam or piece of work is not the end of the world. Even if you mess up, you will probably get another chance to prove yourself, so all you have to do is stay calm and give it your best shot!

- *Make a plan before you begin.* Write down anything you can think of to write about, no matter how stupid it sounds. Write down simple facts such as the people's names and ages you are writing about or important points you must include or what you need to achieve at the end of the piece. It doesn't matter if you are still fuzzy about details and what you are going to write; just get down a basic outline and work from that.

- *Get writing!* Don't just sit there and think, *I have no ideas! Help! What am I gonna do?* Just write an opening sentence and take it as it comes! Even if what you write is not very interesting or is not as you had hoped, you will still get points for spelling and structure (how you set the work out—in paragraphs, for example) and vocabulary (for example, throw in lots of big words that you know the meaning of). You will get more marks for this than if you just sit there for ages worrying about what to put down!

If you try all this and still find that you are having trouble, speak to your teacher. Teachers are there to help you, and they will! Tell him or her about your problem and he or she will probably be able to give you some ideas and help you to tough it!

Also, remember, don't get yourself too worried about this. During high school you will be practicing these skills (writing in class and especially writing to a set time) frequently just so you can work on these skills and learn how to write within a set time. Don't be scared by this. If at first you find it impossible to do, you will practice it so many times that you will be used to it by the time of exams, and it will come easier!

Also, if you freeze up when a project is due, maybe you are nervous because you think that you can't meet the deadline! To prevent yourself from getting like this, just do your projects as soon as you get them so you know that you have lots of time to get them done! Good luck!

—Shannon, 15, England

Doing Your Best in School Activities

What's the Best Way to Run for School Office and Win?

Do you find yourself thinking, *I could do that better*, a lot? Do you want to *do* things, not just talk about them? Do you like staying active? Are you enthusiastic? Are you always solving other kids' problems? Do you have the guts to ask your fellow students to vote for you? If you said yes to any of these, then run for school office!

How to Run for a School Office: Fast-Track Campaign Strategy

- Find out what student officers do. Read the job description before you run for president.
- Pick the office you want. Like to organize things? Be the Activities Commissioner. Dig sports? Sports Commission!

Want a say in how your school is run? Become the School Board Student Representative.

• Now create your Campaign Platform. That's what you stand for. You must answer the question: How will school be different when I'm (fill in your office)? How will it be better for students? Check out what's on students' minds at your school. What do they think needs change?

Sample Campaign Platforms

• Students come in all shapes and sizes. For equal access for all students, Vote for Dahlia!

• Need new gym equipment? Jump in and vote for Jocelyn.

• Take risks. But not with your safety. For a safe school, vote for Tydell.

• Be more. Get more. Vote for Tina Moore.

Getting It Together

Now do you have an idea for a campaign message? Be sure not to make promises you can't keep. Don't say "Escape School at Lunch" if you can't make good on that promise. The next step is to go get allies, or helpers. Campaigning is work. You need student support . . . and family support. Don't be afraid to ask your friends, neighbors, family, and anyone you know for help.

Save Some Trauma Tip

Don't ask your best friend to run your campaign. It will look like you're starting cliques. You run it. Have all your friends help. Be tough: If you can't get six kids to be on your campaign staff and promise to work, don't run yet. Another choice is to serve on some committees and let kids see that you are a leader. Find a teacher who will advise you but stay neutral. Graphics and arts teachers are great friends to make. So is the drama or speech and debate coach at your school.

Make a Powerful Play

Head to the school Student Activities office. Get the forms you need. What rules does the school have on campaigning? Do they have rules about size and number of posters? Or amount of money you can spend? Lots of schools have restrictions because often the student who spends the most money buying everyone pizza will win. That's because the kids feel obligated.

Want to see a great campaign at work? Head here to Tobacco Free Kids: tobaccofreekids.org/youthaction/mission/.

The site has great ideas. There's a cool button, activities like the Art Contest and Kick Butts Day to do, and celebrity spokeskids like Ben Savage and Larisa Oleynik. Spice it up with free poster giveaways, and you've got a great campaign, too.

So how do you get this kind of attention? Here are some ideas:

- Make up a catchy flyer that tells students about you and your ideas.

- Make up a fun button. Pick colors that are your colors so kids identify those colors with you.

- Try to go to club meetings. Give out your flyer, and try to get the support of club presidents. Go to sports practices and do the same thing.

- Have a table and give out flyers when kids are coming to school.

- Attach your flyer to something kids like that's cheap, like a pencil or eraser.

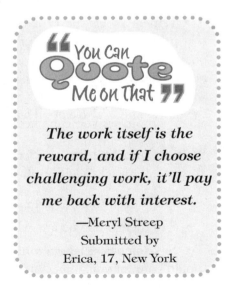

You Can Quote Me On That

The work itself is the reward, and if I choose challenging work, it'll pay me back with interest.

—Meryl Streep
Submitted by
Erica, 17, New York

- Take surveys. Ask students what they want that's different.
- Meet every kid and tell them their opinion counts with you.
- Find the kids who ran for office last year. Talk to them. What worked and what didn't work when they campaigned?

Work It for Votes
- Have a lunch bench party to "press the flesh." (That means shake hands and meet kids.)
- Invite club leaders for cookies or candy.
- Call around and get some free entertainment for your event. There are lots of musical groups, magicians, and clowns who will work for free because they like kids.
- Is there a local sports hero, kids book writer, or star? Invite that person. (Check with your school first!) You'll really stand out and prove your ability to get things done. Then stand up before the entertainment, welcome everyone, and tell them what you will do if they elect you. Make it short. Get back to the party. This is also a good way to rehearse your speech.

Writing Your Speech
Tips from girls who've been there:
- Don't even think of "winging" it. That never works.
- Tell them who you are, what office you are running for.
- Say something about what you believe in and why they should vote for you.
- Tell them what you'll do to make your school a better place for kids.
- Keep it short.
- Make it fun and funny.
- Ask them for the job.

- Look over your speech to see if it is persuasive.
- Read the paper and get ideas from advertisers.
- Say things like, "I'm the candidate you've been waiting for . . . Don't settle for second best."
- And don't forget to say "Thank you!" at the end.

Giving Your Speech

- Don't try to memorize your speech. But practice it a lot before the rally.
- Give a copy to your friend, just in case you lose it.

WRITING A SPEECH?
Matt's Speechwriter has everything you could ever need to write a speech for school or whatever.
www.geocities.com/Area51/Lair/8462/speechmain.html

- Bring a copy with you.
- Dress for success. Look your best when you go up.
- Wear your campaign colors.
- Feel scared? It's okay. Take deep breaths.
- No matter what, just do it. Look at the whole student body before you start to talk.
- Know your speech so well that you know exactly what to say.
- Be confident and enthusiastic.
- Don't just read. Look up every once in a while and make eye contact.
- Don't rush it!
- Do something unexpected in the middle, like a magic trick. Or you could bring a prop, such as a top hat and cane. But don't drop it, or trip, or do anything too weird. No one will forget that.

- Don't bring house pets or anything live as props. Everyone will pay attention to that and not you.
- Have a sense of humor. Don't be totally boring.
- Short is really, really good. Short and to the point is best.
- Don't forget to say thanks.

Election Day

- Remind the kids the day before to vote for you.
- Put out a fresh flyer if you have time.
- Think about what you will do if you win or lose. Practice it in your mind.
- Whatever happens, don't forget to thank the adults and kids who helped you with the election.
- Don't be all mad and upset if you lose. Kids will be watching to see what you do.
- Be cool and congratulate your opponent.
- If you win, smile and say thank you. Thank your staff. Invite the losers to be part of your team. They're leaders, too. Together you can make a real difference.

Tips for New ASB (Associated Student Body) Officers

Did you win? Great! You have a whole new set of challenges. Now you get to do the things you promised. Be the leader you promised to be! Listen carefully to all students when they talk to you. Be a bridge builder. Bring lots of kids into your circle. Don't let the ASB turn into a clique. Stand up for kids who get teased or made fun of. You'll win a lot of respect, and kids will vote for you next year!

Didn't Win? Tips for Next Time

There's always next year! Don't wait; get ready now. Volunteer to be the assistant to one of the people who won. Do it right away! You can also just work on every student activity you can. That will give you experience. And kids will get to know you. Then you can put the promises in your speech to work.

—Written with advice from Emily, Lisa, Erin, Roxanne, Tera, Lorissa, Kendra, Veronica, Katelyn, Jamila, Kela, Susan, and Erica

What's the Best Way to Get a Part in the School Play?

1. Get Ready

• Find out the day of the audition. How many parts will there be? Pick two you really want. Then find out what you have to prepare—a song? dance steps? a scene? Do they give out the scenes (also called "sides")?

• Think about who your characters are and why they act the way they do. Be able to tell someone else (the director may ask you!).

• Next, learn your scene. Also learn a monologue (that's a scene you star in all alone). Be ready to perform it at any time.

• Stand out! Work your scene in front of a mirror. Make sure you have lots of expression. Be able to look really happy, sad, mad, and lots of other emotions. Watch old movies on TV, and ask, "How did the actor do that?" Practice your own acting skills.

• Get together with friends to analyze scenes—but don't audition with a friend; you want to stand out on your own.

Journalize It!

No More Boredom Blues

Are you always trying to figure out something to do at the last moment? Instead of waiting for something to do, list ten activities that you like to do. Make five of them stuff to do when you're alone and five with one or two friends. Now, next time you are bored, look here on your list. And have fun!

Activities to Do Alone

1. Read/Research
2. Exercise
3. _____ Comp.
4. _____ Stories
5. _____ Volunteering

Activities to Do with a Friend or Two

1. Play _____
2. Go to movies
3. Go swimming
4. Pl_____
5. Talk!

2. The Audition

- Wear something brightly colored that stands out. Review your lines before you go up.

- Be ready to let the director tell you what to do. Follow directions. A star is somebody who can make the director believe the line. You won't get the part if you're fussy or hard to work with.

- Be ready to do your lines with other characters.

- Be ready to do a different character. The director may decide you're perfect for another part.

- When you read or say your line, look at the actors you are working with, not at your script.

- Don't be afraid to move. Be animated. If the director says "to project," that means be louder.

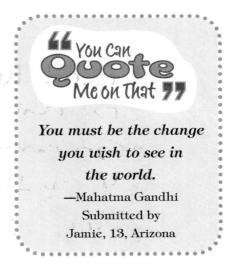

You must be the change you wish to see in the world.

—Mahatma Gandhi
Submitted by
Jamie, 13, Arizona

- Learn how to push your voice to fill the whole theater without getting tired.

- If you don't get the part, ask to be an understudy. Ask to help on the crew, too.

- Don't give up. Take more acting classes and just do your best.

—Written with advice from Kana M., Monica M., Erin Y., and Lorraine Y.

Journalize It!

A Picture Is Worth . . .

Ever feel uncomfortable in school pictures? Everyone does. Try this. Draw your ideal school picture in the box below. Then surround that picture with words that describe the real, wonderful you and the kinds of things you do. Kind. Fun. Adventurous. Curious. Great friend. Discover how you're beautiful on the inside as well as the outside. That's what really counts!

What's the Best Way to Start a Club and Keep It Running?

Starting a club can be lots of fun. It's great to get to plan things and do things for yourself. But it can be hard to get help and keep things going. If you want support for your club, form it at school. Why? Here are several reasons:

- At school, you get a place to meet that's safe.
- At school, you get support, like copies and sometimes money for activities.
- At school, you can do official things, like fundraising and bake sales so you can take a trip.
- At school, you also get recognition.
- At school, you can ask speakers in.
- At school, you can get more members—all the students at your school!

Steps to Take

- Get permission from your school.
- Recruit members who are students at the school; no outsiders, sisters, or neighbors.
- Find an adult advisor, probably a teacher.
- Select a club name.
- Define your purpose, which answers these questions: Why do you meet? What's the club about? If they don't have one at your school, you might start an Honors Club, Student Council, Pep Club, Astronomy Club, or 4-H Club. You might also start a Scout Troop. Here are some ideas for clubs:

  Drama Club
  Country Music Club
  MTV Club

Journalize It!

Members Only

Have you ever started a club or been a member of a club? Draw a picture of you and your club mates here. Do you wear special T-shirts? Have a special symbol? What's your clubroom like? If you haven't started a club yet or been in one, make up your own club today on this page.

Outdoors Club
Hiking Club
Christian Youth Club
Peacemakers Club
Computer Club
Amnesty International Club
Cooking Club
Pet Club
Future Leaders Club
Chess and Strategy Games Club
Academic Olympics Club
Honors Club
Book Club
Art Club
Photography Club

- Arrange for a regular meeting time, like every week. Ask the school to give you a place to meet. Think up an activity to help get started and recruit members—such as a pizza party, ice cream giveaway, etc.

- Create a goal that students can do together, such as have a Shelter Pet Adopt-a-thon, Pet Show, Bike and Skate Rally, or Weird Science Fair, or build a Haunted House.

- Put flyers everywhere. Invite students. Tell teachers. See if you can put an announcement in your school paper.

What the Advisor Does

The advisor makes sure you know about and follow all the rules of the school. She or he will also give directions and help you plan. Your advisor will probably attend your meetings and activities, to help keep you focused and have fun. Ask your advisor to help you get speakers and school money for activities and projects. She or he can also help you plan activities, or maybe a fundraiser to do fun things like take trips. Your advisor can also help you advertise your club events by using school supplies to make flyers and posters.

Running a Club

Don't forget, if you're in charge, you have to show up for the meetings. Be enthusiastic.

Have ideas on what to do, but let other kids speak and do, too. The idea is for everyone to get involved and have fun, not just the officers. If you're doing more than 25% of the work, you need more members or to share more of the job. To be a good leader, stay neutral. Don't pass judgment. Keep good records and be organized. Smile. A good sense of humor helps.

— Written with advice from Erica, 10; Patricia, 16; Kate, 13; and Tessa, 16

What's the Best Way to Get "In" and Hang with the Hotties?

The Problem Dear Being Your Best: I'd like to get in with the "cool" group of kids at school. How do I do it?

— Tawny, 12, USA

A Solution Dear Tawny: Whatever group you would like to be in, here are some basic rules:

- Smile, be happy, and show that you are your own fun, exciting, unique person!

- Don't be shy. Make a new person feel welcome and show them around your school. Make conversation with people you don't really know.

- Volunteer. Raise your hand to be in the school play if it's what "cool" people at your school do, and don't be afraid.

- Be helpful. If someone drops her or his books, then be the first to pick them up.

- Check out that crowd. For a day, take mental note of what the cool people do and then think about it. Do you like this group? Are they a lot like you? If yes, then you'll feel good about hanging out with them.

—Brittany, 11, USA

What's the Best Way to Prepare for an Audition for Band or Chair Test?

If you want to try out for band, you've got to have confidence in yourself. It doesn't matter if you make a mistake. Everybody makes mistakes. Practicing is always the best you can do to sound perfect. As the saying goes, "Practice makes perfect."

Try to pick two pieces that show off your very best music skills. A solo piece, a concerto, a band march, or fight song is good. Work for 4 or 5 minutes of music. Play at your own level; don't play a higher octave than you're used to. If you don't work with a teacher, tape record yourself and listen to what you are playing. Does it sound musical? Don't audition until you can play without breaks or missed notes. Practice, practice, practice!

—Monica M., USA

At the Audition
- Be ready to play all the major scales.
- Be ready to take a sight reading test.
- If you play more than one instrument, start off with your very best.

Q. Hey, I'm moving to a new school soon, and I'm really nervous about making new friends. How do I do that (make friends), and how do I go about ruling the school?

— Christie, 13, Texas

1 I would first see what clubs you could join. That way you'll find kids with mutual interests right away.

Mostly disagree   Somewhat disagree   Somewhat agree   (Mostly agree)

2 I'd introduce myself to every kid who smiled at me. Just be friendly, and you'll be popular in no time.

Mostly disagree   Somewhat disagree   Somewhat agree   Mostly agree

3 I'd have a big party and invite all the kids you meet the first few days. The ones who show up will probably end up being your best buds.

Mostly disagree   Somewhat disagree   Somewhat agree   Mostly agree

4 I think you should volunteer for every activity or club that asks for help. Let the students know that you are the helpful, "teamwork" type.

Mostly disagree   Somewhat disagree   (Somewhat agree)   Mostly agree

5 Lunch is a social time, so go up to a table full of kids who you think you might like and ask if you can sit with them. If they refuse, you wouldn't want them as new friends anyway.

Mostly disagree   Somewhat disagree   (Somewhat agree)   Mostly agree

- If you blow it, just keep going. Everyone makes mistakes.
- Be ready to play very softly and very loudly or soft and loud.

After the Audition

- If you don't get the chair you want, don't sweat it. Ask your teacher what skills you don't have and work on those. Ask if you can retest in a month or two. Some schools have music coaches for free. Get one if you can.

- If you do get the chair, that's great! If you're first or second chair, try to help your section members improve. Have practice and pizza parties to make working together fun. Get into concert band and jazz and as many groups as you have time for. Try different styles.

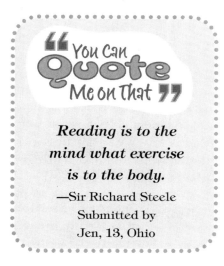

Reading is to the mind what exercise is to the body.
—Sir Richard Steele
Submitted by
Jen, 13, Ohio

—Written with advice from Jennette, 16; Karli, 12; Stephanie, 14; Bryn, 12; and Jessica, 14

What's the Best Way to Get Noticed at School?

The Problem Dear Being Your Best: At my school the kids walk past me like I'm invisible. I'm friendly, but it's like I don't exist. Whassup with this, and how can I make them notice me?

—Alice, 14, Rhode Island

A Solution

Dear Alice: Getting noticed at school is something we all want, no matter how ashamed we are to admit it. Whether it's by a special guy or by the popular kids, we all want attention. However, coming into school with a gigantic nose stud is not the only option. Here are ten ways to have people look at you.

1. **The Walk**: Someone shuffling around with their hands in their pockets is never attention-grabbing, so an ideal way to MAKE people look in the corridors is to perfect the "Look at Me" walk. We're talking supermodel stuff here! In your bedroom, when you have a quiet moment alone, pretend you're on the catwalk. Put your head up, look forward with a determined stare, and think, *I'm gorgeous!* Remember, you don't have to be tall to look tall!

2. **The Clothes**: Let me guess. You've seen girls at school wearing extremely daring, outrageous, but somehow brilliant fashion choices, and never had the nerve to wear something exciting yourself?! Well, it's time you did! Go shopping with a friend who's a daredevil, and look in every shop for something bright and exciting. It doesn't have to be expensive. Make sure it suits you, though! Team it with "the walk" and march into school the next day.

3. **The Attitude**: All this will not work without a strong attitude. So the night before, meditate, sip tea, or do whatever else relaxes you before looking in the mirror with your most cool look and saying, "I'm the best" over and over again until you feel super-cool!

4. **The Talk**: Now that you have the confidence, the power walk, and the outfit, you need the conversation starter for the person you want to notice you. If they are wearing a new piece of clothing, you could compliment them on it. You could also start talking about something simple, yet effective,

like a school subject the two of you hate or a band you both love. Whatever you choose, make sure it's something you can talk about for a while.

5. The Event: This one is the next step. You have the acquaintances; now let's try to make them into friends. At the time of the next big event at your school, like a dance or disco, buy a ticket—even if you have no one to go with. In talking with the new people you know, it's likely you'll find someone who is going, and you can arrange to see them there. If this doesn't happen, you'll probably spot somebody you know once you get there who you can hang with.

6. The Introduction: Now that you know so many new people, you're bound to be introduced, at some point, to the cute guy they hang around with. When you are, don't panic! Talk about usual subjects like music, films, and school. Please don't get into a discussion about sports if you don't know what you're talking about! He might not like sports anyway! By this time, you'll be wearing ultra-hip clothes, so he will notice this. Start talking to him like a proper friend, and soon he may consider you as a girlfriend.

7. The Talent: A big way to get noticed is to let people see your talents. I'm not saying become a show-off, but if you're a singer who's nervous about being in the school show, do it anyway. If you're an artist who's never let the teacher put your paintings on the wall, let them be put up. If you're good at what you do, you might find you receive lots of compliments for it. It also means that next time they're auditioning for good singers, you'll have a good chance.

8. The Conversation Starter: Write an article for the school newspaper or magazine on what you hate, love, etc. People will come up to you and say they agree with your article, and you may be able to use it as a conversation starter for that popular girl you've always been frightened to approach.

46 Chapter 2

9. **The Hangout:** Outside school, start spending time at a popular hangout spot—perhaps a cafe or ice rink. You'll see a lot of friends from school, and new people you'd love to get to know may start talking to you.

10. **The Fun:** Most important of all, have fun being noticed and making new friends. Try to be confident and happy whenever possible, and people will love getting to know you. Attention is something most of us seek but few actually get. With the right balance of clothes, attitude, and talent, anyone can be seen and perhaps even admired.

— Lauren, 14, Scotland

What's the Best Way to Deal with a Pep Squad Tryout?

If you want to try out for cheer, you've got to have confidence in yourself. If you want to be a cheerleader, you should know that it depends on you to bring up the spirit of the crowd, and even the players. As long as the crowd cheers, do whatever you want to put spirit into everybody. La-di-da!

Tryout tip: If you wear some bright colors like yellows and bright reds, oranges, and greens, you feel more vibrant and energetic. I like to do that before I cheer. For surviving, get a good night's sleep and eat a good breakfast and lunch. Always, always stretch. You don't want to pull anything while you are cheering. So remember, eat sensibly and stretch well.

— Tierney H., USA

Get Mental!
- Make sure you are comfortable with the material.
- Be enthusiastic and confident.
- Never try any tumbling or moves that you aren't comfortable with. (Don't try stunts like being a flyer if you've never done that!)
- Make yourself look as good as you can! (Injuring yourself or falling does not make you look good!)
- Get psyched.
- Plan on having fun.
- Do your best and be proud of what you've accomplished.
- Hey, it takes GUTS to try out and perform in public! Don't forget that.

At the Clinic
- Don't bring anyone to the clinic with you. Why? They will be a distraction, and you need your focus.
- Show up early. The practice will start without you! You'll look bad if you come in late.
- Come to practice ready to learn.
- Find out if there is an attendance requirement. Ask: If you miss, will they drop you? Don't be surprised if they do. Half the responsibility of Pep Squad is being there.
- Find out how long the tryouts will be. Sometimes they take up to four days.

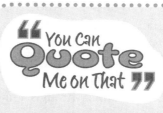

Use what talent you possess: The woods would be very silent if no birds sang except those that sang best.
—Henry Van Dyke
Submitted by
Melanie, 14, USA

I love performing at tournaments, football games, and meeting new people. Plus, we've really become close. Some of my friends feel lost or bored at school. Not me!

—Lindsey L., USA

During the Tryout
Don't bring anyone with you. Your judges are your audience. Be early, dressed, and ready to go when it's time to start. Try to relax and not be nervous. Okay, you will be nervous, but so will everyone else. Above all, act like you're totally having fun.

Smiling is the single most important thing to do during tryouts. Even if you mess up, if you are smiling, chances are that the judges will be watching your face and won't even notice. And if they do notice that you messed up, they'll also notice that you smiled through it and went on like nothing happened. That scores big points.

Good luck!

—Written with advice from Tiffy, 12; Emma, 11; Siobhan, 14; Casey, 14; Jen, 15; and Holly, 13

Why a Person is Not Picked for Pep Squad
- Has poor skills
- Comes late to everything
- Doesn't follow instructions
- Reacts badly to correction
- Can't learn and remember the routines
- Can't keep in place
- Movements and timing are off
- Doesn't mesh well in routines with rest of group
- Has a poor attitude
- Doesn't smile or sell the routine with body language
- Doesn't really seem to want to be doing this

What do I love about Tall Flags? Teamwork. Travel. Times spent together. It's a time I'll remember forever!

—Kathy D., USA

If You Don't Make the Squad

Remember. Twenty-four girls try out; twelve make the squad. That means twelve girls face the disappointment of not making the team. Now what? Don't give up! Schedule an appointment to talk to the judge or the coach. Without anger, ask this person what skills you could improve on to make the team next year. If you are an alternate, go for it! Don't give up! If you didn't make cheerleader, try for dance or drill team or flags. The experience will help, and maybe you'll make it next year.

—Rebecca, 16, Indiana

Developing Your Best Mind

What's the Best Way to Learn a New Language?

How do you learn a new language? Often this can be made really easy if you can be creative. For example, if you study a foreign language, such as I do, link words! You can remember that *kita* means "we" in Indonesian, by remembering the phrase WE fly KITES (kites is like *kita*, get it?). If you let your mind be really creative, you can apply it to all subjects. It's really easy and works! Oh, yeah, and if you massage your feet, the blood going to your brain triples and you can work better.

— Bree M., USA

Tricks to Learning a New Language
Learning a new language is easy if you take it one day at a time. Don't fall behind. Learn one word at a time. Review all the words you learned yesterday today. Then add the new ones. Remember, it's okay to make mistakes. That's how you learn. Above all, remember, you can't cram a language, so don't try.

What's the Best Way to June Up Your Memory?

Have a hard time remembering facts you need to know? You'll improve by practicing, just as you do in sports and other skills. To practice memorization, try these exercises:

★ Read an encyclopedia article about something you really like, such as dolphins. Make a list of ten dolphin facts. Memorize those facts.

★ Take a mental trip to your classroom. How many windows are there in the room? Count them. How many objects can you remember in your classroom? List them.

★ Pretend you are the teacher. What is everyone's name? Go down each row of desks and make a mental list.

How to Own That New Language in Ten Easy Steps
1. Read it out loud.
2. Write it.
3. Cook in it. Seriously! Get a recipe book in your new language.
4. Sing it.
5. Make jokes in your new language.
6. Listen to music in that language.
7. Listen to language tapes.
8. Get together with a friend and play a sport, speaking only that language while you play.
9. Write a movie review in that language and share it with a penpal from that country.
10. Get a penpal (or e-pal!) from another country at: www.agirlsworld.com/geri/penpal/index.html

You Can Quote Me on That

All kids are gifted; some just open their packages earlier than others.
—Michael Carr
Submitted by
Tess, 12, Florida

Never give up. If you have a big, big test, don't sweat it. Study for a couple of hours, then ask someone to quiz you on it. Try to get all the questions right. But if you don't, that's okay. Get to bed early the night before the test so you can get a good night's sleep. The day of the test, just relax and be calm. When you get the test, if you use my tips, I hope you do a good job on your test. And good luck in later years and your life.

— Noell P., USA

—Written with advice from Caitlin, Jess, Sarah, Alexandra, Y.N., Reese, Samantha, and Melissa

Journalize It!

Increase Your Wordpower

Now that most of us are on the Net, it's easy to spend our time surfing or chatting or writing quick e-mail notes. But check out the last e-note you sent a friend. You may find yourself writing, "LOL, u r sooooo cul," which means, "Laughing out loud. You are so cool!"

Shortening words with just a letter or using an abbreviation like LOL is a great "shorthand" way of talking. But in the real world of school and work, no one else may know what you're talking about. Grab a student dictionary and find some interesting words you could use to express how you feel. Write some of your favorite ones down here. Remember, if you "learn a word a day, you will enrich yourself in a hundred ways."

What's the Best Way to Improve Bad Spelling?

The Problem Dear Being Your Best: My spelling is really, really bad. I need a trick to make it better.

—Ashley S, 5th grade, Washington

A Solution Dear Ashley: Everybody has problems spelling. What's worse is when we keep spelling the same word the wrong way, over and over again.

A lot of my friends say that spelling doesn't matter. I think it does. I mean, most girls wouldn't be caught dead wearing jeans to a prom. People would say they are too lazy to dress up. I think bad spelling is like that. When you write, you're putting yourself and what you think down for others to read. When you write things that are badly spelled, you look lazy. It's like you don't care how your thoughts and ideas look to other people. If looks matter, then good spelling matters, too.

GAMEBRAIN
GameBrain is a cool place to find lots of games, games, and more games. Come and check GameBrain out.
www.gamebrain.com/

—Meg, 16, California

Here are some tips to stop that from happening.

Spelling Trouble-Buster Supplies
- notebook you can fit in your backpack
- pencil or pen

Journalize It!

Deal with the Me Inside

Have you ever felt like you're just not smart enough? You try your hardest, but it's just not the best? Write about your experience and how you dealt with your feelings.

- tape recorder and tape
- little student dictionary
- highlighter pen, your favorite color
- reward of your choice, like an ice cream or movie

Step One: Find What You Miss

- Next time you misspell a word, write it down in your Spelling Trouble-Buster Notebook. When you get a test or an essay back with words misspelled, write them down. When you read a word you don't know, add it to the list, too.

- Lots of times, you can't spell what you can't pronounce. Write words down that you can't pronounce.

- If you spell a word a whole new way every day, or if you can only spell part of a word, write that down, too.

NATIONAL SPELLING BEE
There's everything here about future competitions and links to the champions' pages with great ideas on how to spell better. Check it out!
www.spellingbee.com/

- Put a check mark next to words that are in your book already but keep showing up on your papers as misspelled.

Step Two: Catch That Word

Once a week, schedule time to look at your Spelling Trouble-Buster Notebook. Here's what to do.

1. First, pick five words from the ones that have checks next to them. Look them up in your dictionary. Write down their meaning in your book. Put down what kind of word it is. Is it a noun? Verb? Adjective?

Most Likely to Succeed

Doodle a picture of a bunch of words that describe what makes the smartest, best student at school.

Cover up what you've written.

Now ask a friend to do the same.

Compare pictures. What makes up the best students ever? Did you have any of the same ideas? That's cool!

2. Next, ask your mom or teacher to say the first word into your tape recorder. Then ask her to spell that word, slowly, one letter at a time. Finally, ask them to use it in a sentence.

3. Play back the tape to yourself. While the tape is playing, write down the word when it is spoken. Write down the word again when it is spelled out, one letter at a time. Stop the tape.

4. Say the word out loud. Try to pronounce it the same way as you hear it on the tape. Picture the word broken up into syllables. For example: pic ture or bro ken, in to, syl la bles

5. Now start the tape again. Write down the sentence that is spoken.

6. Make up your own sentence using that word. Have someone else check your work to make sure the words in the sentence are spelled right. Make sure the word is used correctly, too, and that the meaning is right.

KIDSNEWSROOM.COM

This site has both fun and news. It is full of entertainment, politics, health, animals, and contests—or you can check out some interactive games.

www.kidsnewsroom.com/

Step Three: Own That Word

Next, have a friend or your parents or someone read your list of five words. Ask them to read the words out of order. Like, bottom to top, or middle of list first. As they read the words, write them down on a piece of paper. Have them check your work to see that the words are spelled right. Highlight the words that are spelled right.

Any word still spelled wrong? Keep taping it, playing it back, and spelling it. You'll get it right. Use the word in a sentence. Make sure the meaning is right.

Step Four: Reward Yourself

Review your list of words every week. Read them over and write them in a sentence. Do a test of these words every four weeks. Got twenty or more right? Highlight them and take yourself out for a movie or a treat!

—Written with advice from Julie, Patricia, Kristina, Laura, Pamela, Emma, Stacy, Allisson, Aisha, and Melody

What's the Best Way to Learn Science?

Eat Brain Food!

Before you study science or math or take a test, eat some of these foods! It's been proven that you will be smarter and remember more if you eat any one of these: apples, pears, grapes, peaches, peanuts, turkey, fish, lean beef, broccoli, and nuts—especially peanuts. You can also drink lowfat milk and eat lowfat yogurt.

—Kate C., 15, Colorado

Tackle Your Science Book

• Get a pen and paper and get ready to survey your reading.

WEBwatch

ANIMAL WORLD

Exercise your curiosity and check out this fun page about animals. It has almost all animals from A to Z with descriptions, information, and even sound.

www.kbears.com/animals.html

- Read your science book very carefully. Don't try speed reading or skimming.

- Stop at a new concept. Write it down. Puzzle it out. Don't be surprised if you don't get a new concept after two or three readings. It's new to everyone at first.

- Look at the topic and chapter headings. You can usually get the main idea by reading these and by looking at any boxes that highlight information.

- Most science texts are like a pyramid—one fact builds on top of the last fact.

- Don't get behind in your reading. Studying science is like learning to play soccer. Skills (and ideas) build every day. Don't try cramming.

- Write down any terms you don't understand. Find out their definitions, or ask the teacher if you don't get a concept.

- Pay close attention to anything in **bold** or *italics*. The author is trying to get your attention!

SCIENCE

Pretend that you're doing your own Dr. Science show. Get a blackboard. Use an empty classroom if possible. Borrow a video camera. Now have each person in the group pretend to be the show host and demonstrate a concept to the rest of the group. Show the tape to your class when you're done. Keep the science real, but be as funny as possible.

You can think up your own experiments, too. Write them down and ask your teacher if she or he thinks they would work. If you need ideas for science projects to try, you can borrow science experiment books from the library. Be sure to ask an adult to supervise when you try the experiments in them.

- Dig through the diagrams and charts or illustrations. Try to get what point they are making. Don't skip any. They usually point out an important concept you'll need.

- To remember more, close your eyes and see whether you can picture the chart in your mind. That will help you remember the information.

GROW YOUR OWN GARDEN!

Here's a science experiment that's fun and tasty! How about growing your own garden! You can find out which gardening tools you need, when to start planting, how to choose seeds, and how to make your garden grow at this site. Grab a friend and plant some flowers. It's more fun to do things together.

www.urbanext.uiuc.edu/firstgarden/

Before Class Starts

- Scan over what you read the day before. If you're lost, don't wait. Immediately ask your teacher for help in the next class.

- Look ahead at the chapter that is next. Get an idea of what the new topic is.

- If your teacher hands out a syllabus (class schedule), glance at it to see where this info fits in.

- Daydream for a moment. Do you already know something about this topic? What do you know?

- Look at the new chapter headings, charts, and pictures. Get a picture in your mind of what the new chapter is all about.

At Home

- Do the homework, even if you don't have to turn it in. Plan to take a 10-minute break for every hour of study.

- Stop if you feel overwhelmed. Give yourself time.

- Getting lost or bored? Talk to yourself! No kidding . . . stop at the end of each paragraph to say out loud what it was about.

- Use your reading to fill in any important facts missing from your class notes.

- Don't highlight or underline bunches of text. Not everything is of major importance.

- Redraw the diagrams and charts yourself. That helps you remember them.

- Stop and review your class notes at least once a week.

BEYOND OUR SKIES: DISCOVERING THE COSMOS
Most of the beautiful things in the universe are stars. If you are interested in stars, then this is the site for you. You can learn about galaxies, stars, and all about astronomy.
library.thinkquest.org/29033/

- Study with friends who like science. Do your homework together and go over what you've learned. Use flashcards to help everyone memorize key formulas and ideas.

- Have everyone in the study group do an experiment or answer a homework question. Then celebrate with a movie or game night.

- Don't forget to tell your teacher about your group. Ask for extra homework or reading or experiments for your study group to do. Your teacher won't forget you when grade time comes around!

Tips and Tricks from Future Scientists Like You!

My favorite lunch to pack: I LOVE pbj's (brain-boosting peanuts and jelly). Peanut butter and jelly sandwiches are really easy to make, and really good!

— Monica M., USA

CATERPILLAR AND MYSTERY BUGS

Not all girls are interested in bugs, but then again, everyone is not the same. This is a site for those girls who do like bugs. You can investigate insects and their relatives, try the tasty bug food, and have lots of fun with bugs!

www.uky.edu/Agriculture/Entomology/ythfacts/entyouth.htm

If you don't understand something, or if you don't get anything you're learning about, this tip is for you: Bring your science book home. Write down problems and have your parents or guardians check it. Talk to your teacher about what you don't understand. Another tip is to get a CD-ROM program like "The Way Things Work" or "Math Blaster" or "Jump Start."

— Kara, 10, Colorado

Contributors of ideas to our Science Busters tips were Paige C., Francia R., Angela S., Kenia V., and Ashley C.

What's the Best Way to Memorize Dialogue in a Play?

Remembering your lines in a play can be pretty scary. If you have a really big part, you may feel overwhelmed! But don't worry, there are things you can do to make it easier.

First, read the whole play. Pay special attention to your part. Figure out how your character moves the play along. What's your contribution to each scene?

Next, keep in mind how your lines build the scene. Make sure you understand the lines around your lines. Make up a substitute line to your lines as you read; improvise it.

The best way to memorize lines is one line at a time. Cover up each line, then repeat it. When you feel good about a scene, cover the lines with paper. Pull the paper down, showing just the cue line. Read the cue line, then respond out loud with your dialogue.

You can also record your scenes on a tape recorder. Be sure to read all the lines, not just yours. Read your lines in a whisper. Say other people's lines in a much louder voice.

Play the recording and say your lines over the whisper when it's time. Next, ask a friend to give you your cue lines. They can fill in if you miss a line.

Problem Solving

If you forget a line, just ad lib. If actors you're working with forget a line, try to cover for them. If they skip pages, try to get them back on track. If you skip a line or pages, just keep going! Try to practice your lines in a mirror so you can check your expressions.

—Rachel, California

What's the Best Way to Tune Up Your Imagination?

- Draw a picture of your future house and everything in it.
- Draw a picture of a space station and all the rooms.
- Draw a picture of the *Titanic* from memory.

Be a Star

What character would you like to play in a play or on TV? Or maybe in a movie? Draw a picture of yourself right here as that character.

- Draw a picture of your favorite scene from a book or a movie.
- Write about your future house and describe everything in it.
- Write about a space station and describe all the rooms.
- Write about the *Titanic*. Pretend you were on the ship. What happened?
- Write about your favorite scene from a book or a movie. Pretend you are the star. What goes on?

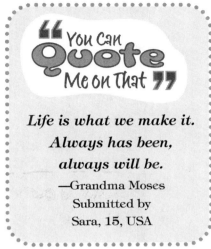

Life is what we make it. Always has been, always will be.
—Grandma Moses
Submitted by
Sara, 15, USA

What's the Best Way to Tune Up Your Sensory Perception?

- Draw a smell map of the route you take home from school. What smells do you pass? Garbage? Roses? Fast food? Chlorine from a pool?
- Make a list of all the textures in your room: Soft wool blanket. Rough wall. Sharp pencils.
- Make a list of all the sounds you heard at school today.
- Try out these five new tongue twisters (and make up some of your own).

A cat catcher can't catch a caught cat.
She gave him a pleasant peasant present.

The sixth sheik's sixth sheep's sick.
Floyd Flingle furiously flipped flat flapjacks Friday.
Six statistics shrink strategies.

What's the Best Way to Tune Up Your Self-Esteem?

- Try a sport you've never tried before. Plan on having fun. Don't worry about being good at it.
- Dress up as your future self in 20, 40, 100 years.
- Try out being President.
- Imagine creating a game. Then make one up. Teach it to your siblings or a friend.
- Create a crossword puzzle.
- Make up your own recipe. Test it on the family.
- Write a story in which you're the hero.

—Tips and ideas for this article contributed by Tasla H., 13; Melissa S., 15; Claudia B., 11; Lindsey M., 9; and Noel D., 16

What's the Best Way to Get Over Writer's Block?

The Problem Dear Being Your Best: I want to be a writer when I'm older. I've already written a rough draft for a story, and I started on another one. Any inspirational ideas to help me when I get "writer's block"?

— Kristel, 12, Ohio

A Solution Hey, Kristel! Writer's block is a very common and annoying problem for us writer types, and probably many people reading this can identify with your problem. I cannot give you specific advice, unfortunately, as to what to write (for example, I cannot say: Write a story about this and call it that and your main characters should be called this, etc.). What I can do is give you some top tips for beating writer's block. Here are six tips:

1. Tip number one is probably the most obvious: Have patience! Don't get frustrated if you can't think of a brilliant idea at first. Be patient and wait for inspiration. An idea for a story or poem can strike you at the weirdest time. You could be cleaning out the hamster cage, washing the dishes, or having a conversation when you get a flash of inspiration. Don't worry, it will come!

2. Try to write a style of story or poem you have never done before. The change of scenery may bring some excitement into your writing and help you get some good ideas.

3. If you are getting bored with a story and can't think of anything else at all to write in it, leave it for a bit and start another. If you are bored just writing your story, the odds are it won't be much fun to read.

4. Try to write something every day, whether it be a chapter of a story, a poem, a song, a letter, a short story, or a diary entry. Whatever! Practicing helps you improve most things, and writing tends to work the same way. Don't worry if you write a whole story just for something to write and then decide it's awful. Can that one! The exercise and experience will do you good as a writer whether you keep it or not.

Book Cover

Draw the cover of the book you'd like to write. Make up a title, and think about who would star in a movie based on your book. Fun!

5. Talk to a fellow writer. Discuss ideas and swap tips for stories and poems, and give each other advice on different ways you might write things, good titles you could use, how to describe things, even ideas for characters' names! You could use the penpal system at AGW for that purpose!

6. Visit writer's Web sites and pick up some tips from them. Use your search engine to find a site for young writers, or try this great site for young writers:

www.cs.bilkent.edu.tr/~david/derya/ywc.html

I hope my tips have been of some use to you. Good luck with the writing, and I hope you get inspired soon!

(P.S. You can also join us on www.agirlsworld.com! There are lots of authors who come to talk in the chat club.)

—Shannon, 15, England

What's the Best Way to Remember Everything?

Meeting Someone
Need to remember a name? Find something about that person's face, body, way of walking or talking, and link it to their name. Here's an example: Mrs. Oxburg has big arms, is strong like an ox, and has white hair like an iceberg! Try using humor or exaggeration as part of the image. You'll remember something a whole lot longer if it's fun or funny or weird.

—Jennifer U., 6th grade, Utah

Think Fast!

Imagine your teacher stops you in the hall and warns you that you're going to have to make a speech in class today. List ten things you could talk about in front of a group of kids for 5 minutes.

Topics I Could Use for a Speech

1
2
3
4
5
6
7
8
9
10

To Remember an Important Task

- Put a rubber band around your thumb and think of the task.
- Put the rubber band around your wrist and think of the task.
- Put a colored ribbon on your backpack and think of the task.
- Turn a stuffed animal upside down beside your bedroom door and think of the task.
- Relax. Nobody remembers anything when they are stressed or nervous.
- When you see these things, you'll remember what you were supposed to do!

—Brianna M., 5th grade, California

Link it Up!

Got a fact you need to learn? Make a link between that fact and something you know really well. The sillier the better. Here's a sample: To learn the capitol of Raleigh, North Carolina, you might link these ideas: I'd love to play "Rally" (for Raleigh) 'round the flag in North Carolina.

—Kari S., 14, Indiana

ARTABUNGA

If you like to draw and play online, then this fun site is where you can let your creative juices flow! You can create your own artwork and send it to your friends, so visit the site.

www.artabunga.com/

Rhymes

Making a rhyme out of information can help, too. Here are some I know:

- "I before E except after C, or when sounded as A as in neighbor or weigh."

- "Thirty days hath September, April, June, and November."
- "Columbus sailed the ocean blue in fourteen hundred and ninety-two."

— Ashley C., Washington

Remembering Lists

Try to make up a joke or a story about a list of things you have to bring to class. If you have to bring a white shirt, sheet music folder, and Beanie Baby collection to a band concert, you might make up a story about a *ghost wearing a white shirt* floating through the air, carrying a *sheet music folder* and swooping down to scare a little kid carrying her *Beanie Baby collection* in a basket.

— Carolina S., 7th grade, California

GIRL ZONE
Exercise your brain in a fun way! Feel like games? One of the best collections for girls is right here! All your favorites: Word Play Games, Arcade, and many, many more!

www.girlzone.com/html/games.html

Visualize

Create pictures to remember things. Trying to remember who discovered radium in a science exam? Imagine where you were sitting and what you were wearing the day you talked about radium. Then try to think of what country that scientist came from. Man? Woman? What was his or her favorite food? What language did he or she speak? Soon your mind may cough up the picture of Marie Curie.

— Whitney T., 8th grade, Nevada

Lost and Found

Ever lose the keys to your house? Try to imagine what you were doing before you last saw your keys. Walk around your house using your mind. Imagine that it is morning and you are going through your routine. What do you see? Hear? Pick up? What were you doing when you last had those keys? Don't want to lose those keys again? Put them in the same spot every day. Then pretend you are taking a mental picture of that spot. It'll be easier to call it to mind next time.

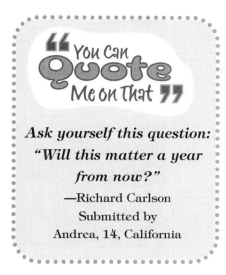

Ask yourself this question: "Will this matter a year from now?"
—Richard Carlson
Submitted by
Andrea, 14, California

— Marlena P., 10th grade, California

Category Cabinet

Learn to group things together in a long list of things you must remember. Like think of all the things you need to brush your teeth. Sink, water, toothbrush, toothpaste, floss, mirror, wastebasket. You can also make groups of dates, famous people, you name it!

— Marlena P., 10th grade, California

Repeat, Repeat, Repeat

An old trick that works is to repeat what you want to remember over and over again. Repeat it out loud. Whisper it. Shout it. Repeat it in your mind. After about forty times, you'll probably remember it!

— Brigitte V., 6th grade, Vermont

Use Your Senses
Sight, sound, taste, smell, and touch are powerful memory tools. Here's how you can use your senses to remember things!

- Highlight the most important points on your notes with the same color pen.
- Draw cartoons or pictures.
- Make charts or diagrams or graphs of facts.
- Talk into a tape recorder.
- Sing your school notes by putting facts in for the words to your favorite song.
- Try listening to Mozart. (Believe it or not, this really works!)
- Try bouncing a ball while you recite facts or lists.

—Carolina S., 7th grade, California

Remember What You Read

- Jot down little notes on what you think is important as you read.
- Review the notes when you get to the end of a chapter.
- Do something with what you just read—such as sing it, bounce a ball while thinking about it, or draw a picture about it.

—Marlene O., 9th grade, USA

Remember What You Learn
If you don't do something with what you learned, you'll forget most of it within a day or two. Here are some ideas:

- Read your notes out loud.
- Talk about the subject with a friend.
- Write a rhyme or poem or draw a picture about what you are studying.

- Think about what you want to remember.

- Visualize what you want to remember.

- Review! At the end of the school day, look over your notes.

- Write for an hour. Then read for an hour. Then take a break.

- Mix up your subjects. Don't do a night of all math and all science.

- Don't cram. Regular study sessions and review help your brain get used to study.

- Pretend to be the teacher and write out your own test. Write the answers, too, and check them later.

—Sheridan M., 10th grade, USA

GET HELP FROM DR. MATH

Hey, Girls and Gals! Need to go for homework help? For net users and Web surfers, check out Dr. Math. Also, AOL members can get special help on homework. Go to Channels, then to Kids Only. Once there, click on Homework Help. From there you can post a question on the teacher message boards, ask a live teacher volunteer a question, explore different things, or look up something in the dictionary. I hope these tips give you some good ideas on how to be prepared and survive school.

—Melody D., USA

Work with a Friend

The Buddy system is the way to go on all studying. Well, at least for me. I remember studying for a HUGE exam on Algebra. It was like in another language for me. So I called my friend Kristen, and she came over and REALLY helped. And as it turned out, I was able to help her study for an English exam.

—Liz R., USA

If you are struggling to learn your spelling or English, this is how you remember things. Say your word is "international." Look at it. Write it on paper. Check it. Then ask one of your parents/sitters/brothers/uncles, etc. to test you. Repeat until you get it right.

—Karyn T., South Africa

What's the Best Way to Memorize Music?

Most teachers feel that musicians give their best performances by playing from memory. That way, you can look at your band director for cues. You don't have to worry about turning pages. And you can give the music the attention it deserves to play your very best.

Steps to Memorizing Music

- Start small, with a short, easy piece.
- Ask your band director to let you make a tape recording of your section playing your music. Or tape yourself playing as you read and play it.
- Listen to your recording a few times. Every piece of music has a shape. It rises and falls, gets louder and softer. Can you "see" the shape?
- Play just the first phrase or a few measures.
- Look away from the music and play it again.
- Play the first phrase over and over until you can remember it without looking at the music.
- Then look at the next phrase or measure.

- Play them again and again.
- Then add them to the music you already know.

Tips for Memorizing Music
- Go slowly.
- Don't do it for hours, or you'll get tired.
- Do it for 20 minutes, then do something else.
- When you come back, listen to the taped music.
- Play the piece by reading.
- Then play it again as far as you can by memory.
- Don't add new measures until you can play perfectly the old ones you've already memorized.

Ways to Really Fix It in Your Mind
- Visualize yourself playing it.
- Hum the tune.
- Try playing your music very slowly.
- Then play it very fast.
- Pantomime playing your music.
- Play it by memory in front of friends so you get used to an audience.
- Ask your band director to let you play it by memory and test you.

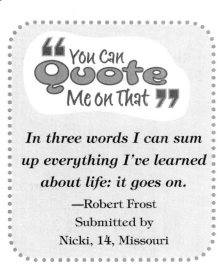

" You Can Quote Me On That "

In three words I can sum up everything I've learned about life: it goes on.
—Robert Frost
Submitted by
Nicki, 14, Missouri

Getting Ready for a Performance

- Play pieces you've memorized again and again. This is called "over-learning."

- Try playing with a radio on or with other musicians in the band playing something different.

- Concentrate on tuning out all the distractions from your mind.

- Try to go in and do a test practice in the same place you're going to perform.

- If you forget a part or mess up, just go on. Probably no one but your band director will notice.

Getting Ready for Music Tests

Practice, practice, practice!

—Laura H., USA

This article was contributed by Amber G., her band director, and members of her school band in Nebraska.

Looking and Feeling Your Very Best

What's the Best Way to Feel Good About Your Body?

The Problem Dear Being Your Best: Lately I've been feeling fat. What should I do to stay fit and boost my energy?

— Oceania, 13, USA

The Problem Dear Being Your Best: People make fun of me, and I can't lose weight. I don't know why. I've tried diets, workout bikes; I've even tried Tae-Bo. Nothing ever works. I would be so grateful if somebody could give me some tips on how to lose weight—and fast, because I have to fit into my party dress before it's too late! My party is next month, and it'll take that much time to lose it! I've got to get rid of it and fast!

— Morgan, 11, USA

A Solution

Dear Oceania and Morgan: Hi, my name is Abby. I never really used to feel good about my body. I would compare myself to really skinny girls in magazines or girls in my class. I'm not fat, but I always thought I was. So I thought that I should give some girls like me a little bit of advice for girls who would like to feel better about themselves.

1. Okay, I know everyone says this, but everyone comes in different sizes and shapes, so accept what your body type is.

2. If it makes you feel better, work out! It made me feel great and more fit after I exercised.

3. Don't compare yourself to super-skinny models. If you do, you'll always end up feeling depressed or not good enough.

4. Eat right! I don't mean cut out cake, cookies, and candy completely; but when you want a snack, instead of pulling out a bag of chips, have an apple or something like that.

5. Last, but not least, stop looking at numbers. It doesn't matter if you're a size 4 or a size 18; if you feel good about yourself and think you look good, great! Scales are just as bad as clothing sizes, too. If you're 98 pounds, don't think you have to be 70 pounds, blonde, and skinny just to look good.

Look at some of the curvier models like Tyra Banks and actresses like Jennifer Lopez. They look like real women. So feel

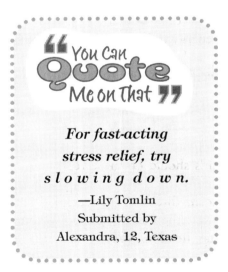

For fast-acting stress relief, try s l o w i n g d o w n.
—Lily Tomlin
Submitted by
Alexandra, 12, Texas

good about yourself, no matter what race, weight, size, or shape you are!

—Abby, 12, USA

What's the Best Way to Tune Up Your Body?

Eat a good breakfast. If you can, bike, walk, or jog to school. Climb stairs. Don't take elevators or escalators in malls. Find out for yourself ten reasons why it's good to be in shape. Decide that you're worth the time and energy to be fit. Don't try to do too much too soon. Don't quit until you've done your exercise program for three months at least. It takes time to see results.

Stop and talk to a teacher if you get dizzy or out of breath. Warm up for 5 to 10 minutes by walking, slow jogging, doing arm circles, or stretching. To get strong muscles, you must use them. Try swimming or lifting weights. (Save the heavy weights till you're 15 or 16. Younger girls should do more repetitions with light weights.)

Push for endurance. That means three times a week for 30 minutes, swim, ride a bike, do calisthenics, jump rope, or do some brisk walking. Stretch. Stay flexible. After you exercise, don't forget to cool down. That's slow walking and stretching. Make exercise a habit. Do a little more every week.

Wear exercise clothing. It should be loose and comfortable. Get a great pair of exercise shoes that fit you. Exercise in the late afternoon before dinner or early in the morning. Don't exercise when it's too hot or humid or within 2 hours after eating a big meal.

Eat healthy food and watch your fat and sugar and salt intake.

—Alyssa, 13, Georgia

Getting in Shape!

Is school about to let out? Soon you'll find a summer full of fun awaiting you. Worried about being in shape? Can you backpack with your family with ease? Bike or swim? Trek the miles across the amusement parks? It's time to get in shape! Make a plan below. Figure out how you're going to fit an hour a day of exercise into your life. Be the best you can be for vacation or school.

Looking and Feeling Your Very Best

Q. I'm 11, and most girls my age wear a bra. I don't. I've asked my parents for one, but they say I don't need one. What should I do?

—Jamie, 11, New Jersey

1 If one of your friends your age wears one, ask her mom to talk to your mom and convince her.
   Mostly disagree   Somewhat disagree   Somewhat agree   Mostly agree

2 Girls develop at different ages. Are you sure you do need one, or do you just want one?
   Mostly disagree   Somewhat disagree   Somewhat agree   Mostly agree

3 Ask if you can wear a sports bra. These look like bras, but you can wear them as a top with shorts, too.
   Mostly disagree   Somewhat disagree   Somewhat agree   (Mostly agree)

4 Tell your mom that you don't care if you are still "flat." There's got to be a bra out there for you, and it's a matter of fitting in with the other girls.
   Mostly disagree   Somewhat disagree   Somewhat agree   Mostly agree

5 Just wear loose-fitting tops so no one can tell whether you are wearing a bra or not.
   Mostly disagree   (Somewhat disagree)   Somewhat agree   Mostly agree

What's the Best Way to Deal with Acne?

The Problem Dear Being Your Best: I have pimples on my face. I am very scared that, because of this, other pupils will not make friends with me.

—Jazmine, 14, Singapore

A Solution Hey, Jazmine! For most people, the decision to make friends with a person is NOT based on whether or not they have acne. However, acne can not only make you self-conscious, but it can also be painful. There are many ways to alleviate the majority of your acne or conceal it. One of the first things you may want to do is schedule an appointment with a dermatologist, or skin doctor. They can give insightful tips on taking care of your face or prescribe specific medications like Retin-A crème, etc. This can be expensive, though, and there are simpler options.

Although acne can be caused by changing hormones inside young bodies, for better skin quality, it is always important to wash your face. You can do this in the morning when you wake up, in the shower, and right before you go to bed. Besides washing with soap or water, there are brand-name medicines available in every supermarket or drug store that you can apply on your face. A caution: Do not overuse these! Many say to use them at the

WEBwatch

ACNE PROBLEM?
Acne Net tells you everything you need to know about acne: how it happens, how to treat it.

www.skincarephysicians.com/acnenet/

most once or twice a day, and if used more, they can damage and scar your skin. Not a good idea! In any case, make it a habit to clean your face twice daily.

Another thing not to do is prod or poke at the pimples or blackheads on your face. The common belief that popping your pimples will "make them go away" is false and can actually lead to scarring. If you've ever seen people with rather torn faces (such as Tommy Lee Jones), you'll understand what I mean. For hiding your acne, you may want to purchase a small kit of concealer make-up at your drugstore. Choose a color that matches your face, and smooth small bits of it over your acne whenever you go out. Remember to wash it off when you get home. Having a concealant may give you some peace of mind.

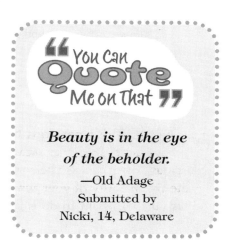

"You Can Quote Me On That"

Beauty is in the eye of the beholder.
—Old Adage
Submitted by
Nicki, 14, Delaware

Lastly, you should remember that often people with acne on their face sometimes get it on their back, shoulders, neck, and upper chest. Neutrogena and other skin care companies offer protection for these areas of your body that you can scrub with every day. You may want to look into prevention care for that sort of thing as well. Anyway, I hope your school year goes great and that you make lots of friends despite your inhibitions! True friends won't worry about a few pimples.

Checklist for Dealing with Acne

- Scrub face twice daily.
- Cut down on high-sugar foods.

Looking Your Best

Summer is coming, and you want to look your best. Below draw a pair of sunglasses that best fit your personality.

Now if you want to make your sunglasses fantasy come true, ask your mom or dad if you can buy some affordable glasses that you can decorate yourself.

- Do NOT poke acne.
- Rinse off face after sports or warm periods of the day.
- Use a skin color concealer to hide especially prominent acne.

—Melody, 13, California

What's the Best Way to Stop Having Bad Hair Days?

The Problem Dear Being Your Best: My hair is a mess. I need to know how to do my hair, like get a list of different hairstyles that are cute and popular now or how to use different clips, etc.

—Ashley, 11, USA

A Solution Dear Ashley: If your parents would let you, try coloring streaks (it all depends on the color of your hair, but most people try blond streaks). All good-looking hair starts with a good cut. If you have long hair and your parents won't let you do streaks, try layering it. If you have short hair, you can do lots of things. You can clip your bangs to one side with a cute butterfly clip. You can gel it all back in a sleek look. If you have shoulder-length hair, you can curl in the ends and make it form to your face.

There are those cute Snap-On gems that make your hair "glitter." If your hair is long enough, you can use a colorful headband or put it up with a ponytail clip. One of the best ways to find a hairstyle is online. It's a lot of fun, too! You can pick the shape of your face and your hair color and see what

Q. My legs are really hairy, but the hair is kind of light colored. My mom won't let me shave. I have tried and tried to convince her. One of the girls at my school even told me to my face that my legs were too hairy. What would you do about this?

— Kayla, 12, California

1 You can always wear colored stockings in the winter, but for summer that won't work. Tell your mom you are embarrassed and that this affects your life more than she thinks.

Mostly disagree   Somewhat disagree   Somewhat agree   Mostly agree

2 If one of your girlfriends your age shaves her legs, ask her to come over with her mom and, together, help you convince your mom.

Mostly disagree   Somewhat disagree   Somewhat agree   Mostly agree

3 If it's the shaving your mom hates, tell her you'll use a hair remover cream or waxing.

Mostly disagree   Somewhat disagree   Somewhat agree   Mostly agree

4 If the hair on your legs is light, why is it such a big deal? Just ignore people who don't like it.

Mostly disagree   Somewhat disagree   Somewhat agree   Mostly agree

5 Show your mom pictures in all the magazines of hair-free girls your age. Have all your friends come over and show her. If she's outnumbered, maybe she'll finally agree.

Mostly disagree   Somewhat disagree   Somewhat agree   Mostly agree

the possibilities are. Here are some Web sites you can try: www.hairdos.com, www.salonweb.com. I'm sure you'll find a style that's right for you!

—Kim, 17, Canada

What's the Best Way to Deal with Sweat?

Don't "Sweat" It? Easy for You to Say!

The Problem Dear Being Your Best: I have a bad problem with sweating. No matter what I do, I can't seem to stop sweating. People tease me because by the end of the day, I have sweat marks under my arms. It got to the point where I only wear white shirts. What can I do about this??

—Allison, 13, New Mexico

A Solution Dear Allison: Some people sweat more than others, but you can do things to help your perspiration. You can see your physician and ask him or her for a strong prescription deodorant/antiperspirant or go to the store and buy an over-the-counter antiperspirant. I suggest that you try different kinds each time until you find the perfect one. Remember to read the

The most wasted of all days is one without laughter.

—e. e. cummings
Submitted by
Elaine, 15, Canada

First Impressions

Ever find yourself making up a story about people you see or just meet? You get a feeling about them. That's a first impression. Try this. Sit down at a mall and do some people watching. Find three people, and just from looking at them, write down your first impressions, based on nothing but their looks. Remember, these are just imaginings. No one can really get the story on someone from first glance.

Impression #1	Impression #2	Impression #3

Now draw a picture of someone at school who you don't know well but who you think you know from looking at or watching them.

What's your impression? Think it's a true one? Or just a story you tell yourself? Try to get to know this person better, and then fill in the blanks. You can't really know anyone from a first impression.

label. You want something to stop the sweating, not just to make you smell good. Be sure the bottle says "antiperspirant" as well a deodorant. If it just says "deodorant," it won't solve your problem.

Also, if you carry a purse or backpack, you can put a stick of deodorant/antiperspirant inside and apply it in the bathroom when needed, or after gym or before. On the other hand, you could wear a heavier material for a shirt, and wear "sweat pads" under your clothes to stop those "rings" on your shirts. Don't be embarrassed. Everybody sweats!

—Suzanne, 13, USA

What's the Best Way to Live and Be Totally Fit?

Hey, girls out there! One of the number one issues teen and pre-teen girls face today is losing weight, and, surprisingly, there are fairly simple guidelines to follow. However, before I outline these fundamental steps to becoming fit, I think it pertinent to name several things that *don't* work and why.

The first is fasting. Many girls try this and shed several pounds, but the weight is easily regained. Why is this? Metabolism. A person's metabolism is defined by how fast they process food, and most girls with weight problems have slow metabolisms. When a person fasts, the body reacts as if the person were unintentionally starving and slows the metabolism even more so that important fats can be stored. Not exactly the picture-perfect scenario for someone who wants to get their metabolism going faster, eh?

Another thing *not* to do: DON'T take diet pills! Many diet pills simply take your appetite away, and there you go again—fasting.

So how do you lose weight without prepackaged food, pills, or fasting? Simple: Change your diet and start a frequent exercise program for yourself.

The easiest way to get your body to shed excess fat is through sweating: Sweating is a by-product of aerobic exercise, which, for best results, should be done for 30 to 40 minutes every day. If you've never pushed your body to work hard, you should start off slowly: Try walking for 10 minutes every other day and add a few minutes each time as you feel stronger, slowly building your endurance. Likewise, if you are starting to jog, start with only 5 to 10 minutes and work up to 30 to 40 minutes, walking when you feel tired.

Exercise is also an important part of keeping your body at a weight that's healthy for your height. When the body utilizes the nutrients in food, it burns the nutrients to provide the body with energy, or calories. Yet, if the body isn't able to use all the calories that are available, it stores them away as fat. Exercise helps burn up excess calories; the body uses them as extra fuel to keep you going.

You most likely already know that the heart is a muscle; it's actually the strongest muscle in the human body. But did you know that, just like other muscles, the heart likes a good workout? You can provide it with an excellent workout in the form of aerobic exercise. Aerobic exercise is any type of exercise that makes your muscles use oxygen. Because aerobic exercise is repetitive, it brings fresh oxygen into the muscles of the body over and over—making the heart muscle stronger (and sometimes a bit larger, as well).

Aerobic exercise increases the number of blood cells in your blood so your blood can carry more oxygen than before. It also helps the blood travel more efficiently through your blood vessels.

You may be wondering what other benefits exercise offers. Are you depressed? Well, aerobic exercise actually plays a large part in a person's mental health. This is because exercising causes the body to produce endorphins or chemicals that arouse the feelings of peace and happiness. Types of exercise requiring deep breathing can also relieve tension, just as people engrossed in high-power sports rid themselves of painful emotions.

Exercise can also help with self-esteem. If you are feeling strong and powerful, it can help you see yourself in a better light. Additionally, the pride of achieving a certain goal, such as beating your old time in the 100-meter dash, can give you a real sense of accomplishment.

It's recommended that teenagers do some sort of aerobic exercise at least two or three times a week, for 20 to 30 minutes at a time. Many teens who play team sports may do even more than what's recommended—and that's great! The heart appreciates it, and you'll be able to do more and more exercise without getting tired. Some team sports that are good for pouring on the oxygen are swimming, basketball, soccer, lacrosse, field hockey, ice and roller hockey, and rowing.

But if you don't play team sports, don't worry. There are plenty of ways to get aerobic exercise on your own or with a few friends. These include biking, running, aerobics, dancing, in-line skating, and fast walking. In fact, types of exercise that you can do on your own are easier to continue for years to come so you can stay fit as you get older.

Curious about how many calories you burn while exercising? Below is a chart of several activities and approximate calories burned in 30 minutes:

Activity	Calories Burned
Volleyball	100
Leisure Swimming	125
Brisk Walking	160
Riding Bike	160
Gardening	185
Tennis	220

Talk Abouts

Q. Lately I feel like no matter what I do . . . I just screw it up! Like there's no point in living anymore. At one stage I was about to jump into the middle of the road, but my friend grabbed me and pulled me back . . . I just don't want to live anymore. What should I do?

—Suzy, 12, New Zealand

1 You sound really depressed. Please talk to a school counselor or adult about getting some medical help as well as counseling. You are only 12. There is a lot to live for!

Mostly disagree   Somewhat disagree   Somewhat agree   Mostly agree

2 You say you screw everything up. Everybody screws up. Don't be so hard on yourself. Concentrate on something that you do enjoy and know you can do.

Mostly disagree   Somewhat disagree   Somewhat agree   Mostly agree

3 Physical activity really helps people who are feeling hopeless feel better. Force yourself to dance or run or swim. I guarantee you'll feel better.

Mostly disagree   Somewhat disagree   Somewhat agree   Mostly agree

4 If you are trying to run into the road, you need serious help. Please tell an adult that you trust how you feel, and ask them to help you before you do something to hurt yourself.

Mostly disagree   Somewhat disagree   Somewhat agree   Mostly agree

5 If you have a friend who pulled you back when you tried to go into the road, then you have a lot to live for. Confide in your friend, and, together, you can improve your feelings.

Mostly disagree   Somewhat disagree   Somewhat agree   Mostly agree

Links to Other Fitness Web Sites

1. www.fitten.com/
Workout charts you can keep, sample workout routines, ideas to fix your eating habits, recommendations for safe weight loss, and more. Share losing weight and getting in shape tips with other teens. Healthy choices and recipes that taste good and are fun to eat!!

2. library.advanced.org/10991/
Nutrition on the Web for teens. This is a source site for exercises, health myths, recipes, diet planning, live chat or e-mail questions about nutrition, losing weight, etc. Can be accessed in Spanish, German, and English.

3. www.vrg.org/nutrition/teennutrition.htm
Want to go Veggie? Good site for advice on a healthy weight-losing diet that excludes meat.

4. www.kidshealth.org

5. www.prcn.org/library/youth/teen.htm

—Article by Melody, 13, California

What Are the Ten Best Ways to Feel Good Inside?

The Problem Dear Being Your Best: No matter what others tell me, I feel overweight, ugly, not too bright, and just overwhelmed with my life. I need to cheer up. What do you suggest?

—Aura, 14, U.S. Virgin Islands

Q. My friends are doing some pretty bad things. Like drinking, drugs, etc. People tell me I should notify their parents, but I don't want to get them in trouble. I know they can be harmed, but they probably would never want to talk to me again. What would you do?

— Avery, 13, New York

1 Continue to hang with them, but show them an example by always saying no thanks to alcohol or drugs.

Mostly disagree   Somewhat disagree   Somewhat agree   Mostly agree

2 Tell your own parents about it and let them decide if they want to tell these kids' parents.

Mostly disagree   Somewhat disagree   Somewhat agree   Mostly agree

3 Plan activities with one friend at a time. Make sure that there is no alcohol or drugs around so the friend can't be tempted.

Mostly disagree   Somewhat disagree   Somewhat agree   Mostly agree

4 You need to stop hanging with these kids. No matter how close you are to them, they are in a lifestyle that you don't want to join.

Mostly disagree   Somewhat disagree   Somewhat agree   Mostly agree

5 You should only tell their parents on a one-by-one basis. If one kid is seriously threatened by his or her activities, then tell that one kid's parents.

Mostly disagree   Somewhat disagree   Somewhat agree   Mostly agree

A Solution

Hey, Aura! These are ten ways that make me feel good about myself when I'm feeling down or forget how great I am. Of course, everyone's different, but I believe there's something in here for everyone. I hope this helps you feel your absolute and very best, as well!

1. Look in the mirror and say to yourself, "I am a special girl and there's no one in the world like me. I can do anything!" Cheesy as it may sound, it actually works!

2. Do something nice for someone. Volunteer at an animal shelter, go visit a nursing home, or maybe just invite that girl who always sits alone at lunch to sit with you. Helping others always makes me feel good.

3. Smile! Be friendly to people you encounter. Look for the good qualities in your friends and family. If you start acting like you're happy and in a good mood, then you soon will be!

4. Go outside! Do something active in Mother Nature. Take a hike, go swimming, or just lay on the grass and watch clouds pass.

5. Do something you're good at! If you love to sing, then go turn on some music and belt it out! Remind yourself how good you are at so many things!

6. Learn something new! Broaden your horizons! Have you always wanted to learn how to dive or to learn sign language? Go for it! New challenges are fun and give you a sense of accomplishment when you've finished!

7. Start a diary. Write down your thoughts, dreams, goals, poems, or anything you want! Writing always helps me express my feelings.

8. Read! Read a nonschool book just for fun. Lay off of the TV and let your imagination soar!

9. Hang with your family! Have a bonding-fest with Mom or Dad or maybe even a sibling. We all need that quality family time.

Chapter 4

Journalize It!

Doodle

Draw a picture of yourself in the most fashionable outfit you can imagine.

10. Venture out on your own a little bit! Be a leader! If you have an awesome routine but none of your friends are entering the talent show, enter anyway! Show everyone how creative and unique you are!

—Gabriella, 15, Arizona

What's the Best Way to Learn About Fashion Fast?

I researched and I came up with 20 top fashion and beauty sites. Here they are!

1. www.lasenzagirl.com
2. www.bluefly.com
3. www.gap.com
4. www.tops.co.uk
5. www.girlzine.com
6. www.fashiontrip.com
7. www.cosmogirl.com
8. www.hifriend.com
9. www.lifeenergyintelligence.com
10. www.zenq.com
11. www.hip-hat.com
12. www.jump.to/swerve
13. www.theteenzone.com
14. www.teenfashionworld.com
15. www.girlslife.com
16. www.jumpinjammerz.com
17. www.covergirl.com
18. www.bonne-belle.com

Q. There is a dress code at my school. And I do obey it. But everyone says I dress in clothes that are too tight. I can't wear baggy stuff 'cause I am too thin and would look like a bag lady. How can I tell them that I AM obeying the code and get them off my back?

— Ashley, 13, USA

1 As long as the school officials aren't on your back about it, just ignore these people.

Mostly disagree   Somewhat disagree   Somewhat agree   Mostly agree

2 How "tight" is "tight"? If you are wearing stuff that looks three sizes too small, consider getting a bigger size.

Mostly disagree   Somewhat disagree   Somewhat agree   Mostly agree

3 You say you are "thin." Maybe they are larger and are jealous. Just ignore it.

Mostly disagree   Somewhat disagree   Somewhat agree   Mostly agree

4 Ask your parents if they think you look okay. If they think your clothes are too tight, maybe there's a problem.

Mostly disagree   Somewhat disagree   Somewhat agree   Mostly agree

5 Is it girls or guys who are saying your clothes are too tight? If it's girls and the guys think you look great, why change your outfits?

Mostly disagree   Somewhat disagree   Somewhat agree   Mostly agree

19. www.sketchers.com
20. www.girlzone.com

I hope girls all over the world will enjoy these sites!!! Bye! Love,

—Zara, 12, England

What's the Best Way to Try Modeling?

Hi. My name is Xena, and I am 12 years old. I'm writing to tell you about my modeling madness. When I was 7 years old, I started modeling with a small agency. They didn't get me any work, so I started modeling at my school, but that was not enough for me; I needed more. So I decided to look for an agency on the Internet. My luck was up, and at the age of 11, I had found a good agency. I've stayed with them since then and I am now on my second-to-last course, which is photographic. I attend modeling classes every Wednesday, and I have made a lot of friends—all thanks to my computer. But that is not all. Here are a few sites for all of you modeling-madness people like me.

> www.modelingadvice.com
> Want advice about modeling? This site is called Modeling Advice, and it has all kinds of areas to check out: What does it take to be a model? How do you find work? What's expected during a photo shoot? What does "working the camera" mean? How can you prepare to be a model? There are also great sections on photographers, links to agencies, and even modeling scams.

BODY WISE

Your body is yours and nobody else's. Love your body, and if you're not too happy about it, here is a cool, fun site to help you out! There are great places on how to get fit, what body image you have, and how to eat right and get all your essential vitamins.

www.girlpower.gov/girlarea/BodyWise/index.htm

www.newfaces.com/supermodels
I recommend you look up New Faces/Supermodels. This site has all you want to know about your favorite supermodels, how to become a model, what's in style NOW, and much, much more.

modelnetwork.com/home/index.html
The Model Network site is for all those future supermodels! Wow. This site includes agents for children's modeling, television commercial agents, and lots more. I hope you enjoy these cool sites, and good luck with your future modeling career!

— Written by Xena, 12, South Africa
Edited by Irina, 12, Argentina

Performing Your Best in Sports

What's the Best Way to Pick a Sport to Play?

The Problem Dear Being Your Best: I'd like to compete in sports but don't know which one is best for me. I'm strong, have quick reflexes, but I wear glasses. I like team sports but don't want to be the captain of anything. Any suggestions?

—Rona, 14, Utah

A Solution Hey, Rona! Choosing a sport is a funny thing. It's hard to give advice on. You just have to try any that look fun. Your glasses shouldn't interfere with your playing, unless it's a full-contact sport like basketball. For those sports, you can buy special glasses that have a strap around your head so they don't fall off.

You say you have quick reflexes? Maybe the all-American sport of baseball is the way to go. There's not a whole lot of contact, so your glasses shouldn't get in the way, and your

quick reflexes could give you an advantage if you play infield. So get out there! Sign up for everything you can get to! Hey, it can't hurt just to try, but get ready to work!
   Good luck!

—Lindsay, 15, Louisiana

What's the Best Way to Deal with Refs?

The Problem Dear Being Your Best: What's the best way to deal with refs when they are wrong? Why can't you argue with any refs in sports? Sometimes they are really wrong! Who are refs responsible to? Who can throw one out if he or she wasn't fair?

—Tessa, 13, Canada

A Solution Hey, Tessa! I completely understand your feelings! It can get really aggravating when a referee makes a bad call and there is nothing you can do about it. But unfortunately, there isn't really anything that can be done about that. A coach can try to argue a point with a ref, but the ref has authority over the coach, so what he or she says goes! I don't think a ref can be thrown

PICK YOUR PERFECT SPORT!

Want to know what sport is right for you? Take this quick 10-question quiz and let the Women's Sports Foundation help you figure out which sports might be perfect for you!

www.womenssportsfoundation.org/cgi-bin/iowa/sports/ggg/find.html

out of a game unless he or she physically harms a player or coach.

However, if you believe a referee is treating one team unfairly, you can appeal to the Athletic Department, and they can take action. I hope this helps you! Just keep in mind that the sole purpose of a ref is to have everyone play fair, even though sometimes they make you mad!

Have fun and good luck.

—Lindsay, 15, Louisiana

What's the Best Way to Deal When You're No Good at Sports?

The Problem Dear Being Your Best: I'm not good in sports. Right now it matters to me because in gym class we're doing a lot of exercises that I don't really know how to do, and I want to do better in sports. I'm too lazy to practice at home! Please give me some useful advice!

—Shir, 13, Israel

A Solution Hey, Shir! Well, not everyone is graced with the natural talent of being athletic. And gym

If I accept you as you are, I will make you worse; however if I treat you as though you are what you are capable of becoming, I help you become that.

—Johann Wolfgang von Goethe
Submitted by
Laurie, 15, Canada

Q. I'm really into the sports softball, swimming, and football. Well, I've got the rep of being a tomboy. I try hard to be more of a girl, but no one takes me seriously. Do you have any tips for me on how to become more of a girl?

— Marcelle, 13, New Jersey

1 Hey, just because you like sports doesn't mean you aren't a girl! Just be yourself. You don't have to act "girly" to be taken seriously.

Mostly disagree   Somewhat disagree   Somewhat agree   Mostly agree

2 If you want to be more of a girl, don't drop your love of sports, just try cleaning up a bit and wearing a little bit of makeup and more feminine clothes.

Mostly disagree   Somewhat disagree   Somewhat agree   Mostly agree

3 Ask your mom to give you some advice on how to seem more feminine. It could be something as simple as a new hairstyle.

Mostly disagree   Somewhat disagree   Somewhat agree   Mostly agree

4 Ask some of your guy friends what they look for in a girl, then go out and become it!

Mostly disagree   Somewhat disagree   Somewhat agree   Mostly agree

5 Find some girls that you admire and copy their style and mannerisms.

Mostly disagree   Somewhat disagree   Somewhat agree   Mostly agree

class can be a real pain. But that same wornout phrase that practice makes perfect is still the best advice any athlete can get. There are other ways to practice than running five miles a day or doing 200 push-ups.

Try just pulling out your bike and riding around the yard (the grass creates friction and you get more of a workout). There are tons of fun exercises you can do that will make those pesky gym classes less strenuous. If you live in an apartment building or a two-story house, take the stairs. The lifting of your body weight on your legs will keep them strong, and you'll seem lighter when you are just walking. If stairs aren't an option, walk. It's easy (you do it every day!), and you can see the world in 3-D instead of on the TV.

If you are looking for something with a little more of a workout, calisthenics never failed anyone. Jumping jacks, squat thrusts, toe touches, and even the dreaded push-ups and sit-ups can all help you not to become a full-fledged couch potato. If, as you say, you're "too lazy" to practice at home, doing some of these things with friends to your favorite dance or pop tunes can be fun for all of you and won't seem like "work." I'm sure you have at least one or two friends who feel as you do. If you want more exercises, talk to your gym teacher, and I'm sure he or she will help you out.

Good luck and keep in shape!

—Lindsay, 15, Louisiana

GIRL GYMNASTICS!

This is a great site to see all the different aspects of gymnastics and explore Bela and Martha Karolyi's gymnastic camp. It will show you many things used in gymnastics and give you helpful hints.

www.girlsgymnastics.com/

Winning Takes Imagination

Draw a picture of yourself winning a trophy or a championship in your favorite sport. If you can dream it, you can do it. You go, girl!

What's the Best Way to Fit into a Team?

The Problem Dear Being Your Best: Hi! I'm pretty much the whiz at any sport. You name it, my coaches say I play like a pro. But my team players think I play way too tough. What should I do?

—Priscilla, 12, Arizona

A Solution Hey, Priscilla! Well, first, I have to say that it's really great that you are such a good athlete! I'm not really great at any sport, so I know where your teammates are coming from. It can be pretty intimidating to be just starting out in sports and have a really good player throwing a ball at you, or whatever. My advice is to take it slow. You might be a strong player, but if your teammates can't catch your passes, then it won't do any good.

Just be considerate of the players you are interacting with. If it's a girl you know isn't a strong player, be gentle with her. Don't scare her to death by throwing or hitting your hardest! So take it easy on other players. Once they get used to playing with you, then they'll get stronger and your team will be one of the best! Good Luck!

—Lindsay, 15, Louisiana

JUMP INTO SNOWBOARDING
This is an awesome site to get you off your feet and onto a snowboard. It has everything from the history of snowboarding to the right equipment to interviews, and much more.
tqjunior.thinkquest.org/3885/

How Can I Play My Best Game on an All-Boys Team?

The Problem Dear Being Your Best: I am now playing basketball on an all-boy team. How can I block them without them thinking I am flirting?

—Jenny, 15, Florida

A Solution Hey, Jenny! I think it's great that you are talented enough to play on a team composed of only boys except yourself! As for your question, I think that after your teammates or opponents get over the shock of seeing a girl playing with them, they won't think anything of your blocking them. If you stay serious about the game, they won't think you are trying to get close to "flirt," but that they'd better keep their minds on the game or your team will win!

This is a timeless obstacle that women for centuries have tried to overcome in every field, whether sports or business. Most of the time, in man-dominated subjects, such as the medical field (50 years ago a woman doctor was almost unheard of!), it's hard for a girl to have any real impact. But it has happened, so just stick in there! Ignore what some other players might say to try and rattle you to make you quit, and just play your heart out!

Good luck!

—Lindsay, 15, Louisiana

> **" You can Quote Me on That "**
>
> *Without a struggle, there can be no progress.*
> —Frederick Douglass
> Submitted by Kelley, 12, Canada

Journalize It!

Looking Up To

Everyone needs heroes. So who are your sports heroes and role models? List your top ten heroes here. Then list what makes them so great.

1.

2.

3.

4.

5.

6.

7.

8.

9.

10.

What's the Best Way to Boost My Skills?

The Problem Dear Being Your Best: I really want to play baseball, but I'm not that good at it. I know most of the rules. What are some of the ways I can boost my skills?

—Shekelia, 12, Georgia

A Solution Hey, Shekelia! As always, I think it's great that you want to play baseball! My sister plays all the time, and she is awesome at it. I play league ball, but baseball doesn't come as natural to me as it does to my sister. So I have had to practice really hard to sharpen my skills at the game. Why don't you try asking a parent or sibling or friends just to play catch with you? Practice makes perfect, but who says it has to feel like practice? Make a game out of it.

Exercise your body by having someone hit to you, not just throw the ball to you. Move around, make your reflexes work for you. Ask a coach to teach you the proper batting stance, and have someone pitch to you. Don't have anyone to play with? Hitting off a T-stand (you know, like the ones they use in T-ball) can help you with your swing.

There are lots of ways to build yourself up for the game, but the best tip I can give is this: Have fun! It's just a game, and besides, you'll play better if you enjoy it!

—Lindsay, 15, Louisiana

> **WEBwatch**
>
> **GIRL'S SOCCER WORLD**
> Want to find out how to be your best at your next tryout? There are great tips here!
>
> www.girlsoccerworld.com/refs/coaches.html

What's the Best Way to Deal When You Don't Make the Team?

The Problem Dear Being Your Best: Hi. In 6th grade, I tried out for cheerleading. I did not make it. I made it every year before that. I have always been in some type of cheerleading. If I don't make it this year, I'm going to have a nervous breakdown. What can I do to learn how to do better jumps and learn how to do flips?

— Danielle, 12, Texas

A Solution Hey, Danielle! Despite all of the jokes made about cheerleaders, it really is hard work. I know. I've tried out before, and you have to be really athletic, especially in junior high and high school cheerleading. Now just because you don't make it one year doesn't mean you won't ever get back on. Here are three tips I dug up on how to be a better cheerleader:

1. *Keep working.* The girls who did make it will be doing it all year, so you need to keep in shape. Stretch your legs and arms really well and long before attempting all those jumps and flips. If you pull a muscle, then it will be a little hard to try out!

2. *Talk to other cheerleaders.* You must have made friends while you were on the squad, so talk to the girls who made it this year. Ask them for tips, and practice with them at their houses. There are all kinds of little things that cheerleaders have to do besides jump and yell.

3. *Keep your ears open for cheerleader workshops.* When I was in grade school, I can't remember how many cheerleader camps I went to! Pay attention to your local newspapers, and talk to teachers who sponsor your high school squad. Those camps aren't put on just to raise money; you could really get something out of it!

I hope these tips help you. Just remember, though, that it isn't a popularity contest (although it does seem that way sometimes), and just because you don't make it doesn't mean that you can't try something else. There are other clubs and sports you can join, so keep an open mind. You don't have to be a cheerleader to be happy!

Good luck!

— Lindsay, 15, Louisiana

What's the Best Way to Begin Track?

The Problem Dear Being Your Best: I want to know if I should be in track. The only reason not to is that there is this guy on the track team, and if he sees me run, I think he might think I'm awful or something. Help please! I really like track, but I like this guy, and I don't want to make a fool of myself!

— Amber, 14, Maine

A Solution Hey, Amber! The only thing I can think to tell you is just to be confident in yourself. I know you might feel all funky when you run, but that's just in your head. However, if you still want to learn the "proper" way to run, this is what I was taught when I ran track:

1. *Pump your arms.* When you run, your arms are going to swing. It's simple physics! But there is a way to swing your arms so that you don't end up smacking yourself in the face! When you step with your right foot, bring your left arm up. Bend it a little at the elbow, and don't clench your fist or flex your hand. Swing your arm so that your palm ends up almost even with your right ear. Then alternate when you run: left leg, right arm;

right leg, left arm. You don't have to overexaggerate either, just do what's comfortable for you!

2. *Don't kick your legs up.* When you run, try not to do a butt kick. I don't think that's what your problem is, but I've seen some people do that, and it looks crazy! In addition, try not to land flat-footed. Keep your heels up, and stay on your toes. It'll help you go faster and not make that embarrassing slapping when you run!

3. *Breathe.* Inhale through your nose and exhale through your mouth. It'll help control your breathing so you don't pass out while you're running. You won't end up looking like a dog with your tongue hanging out!

Well, Amber, I hope this can help you not to feel so silly when you run! In addition, just remember to be confident in yourself. If this guy is for you, then he'll like you regardless of how you run!

—Lindsay, 15, Louisiana

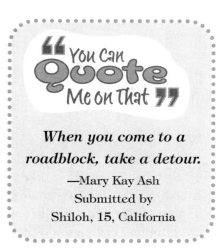

When you come to a roadblock, take a detour.

—Mary Kay Ash
Submitted by
Shiloh, 15, California

How Do You Get the Best Out of Your Sports Tryout?

First things first. You need a winning attitude. That means:
- Be determined.
- Want to win.

- Stay strong and fast.
- Build your endurance.
- Don't slack.
- Support your team; don't play with Gameboy on the bench.
- Go to practice feeling like "my sport rocks"!
- Have high expectations, and meet them.
- Make your goal to improve every day.
- Start out strong, and keep the momentum going.

— Danielle R., 12, Basketball, USA

What It Was Like: Trying Out for Basketball

When we showed up, we each got a number to pin to our shirts. Then the coaches divided us into groups of ten players on each half court. We worked as a group the whole time, first stretching, then jogging around the gym. Then the coach set us up to do drills. We did full-court weaves and passing drills. We did dribbling drills around the cones and across the court. We did defensive drills and one-on-one drills. Then we showed our shooting hoops skills and did a few practice scrimmages.

Then the coaches had a huddle. They mixed up the scrimmage teams, and we got to play four 10-minute games, changing the positions of players every game. They took notes the whole time.

The next day, they posted the numbers of the kids who made the team and the alternates. I didn't make it this year. But I am going to try out for volleyball because I'm in good shape and they need more players. Maybe I'll make basketball next year.

—Jessica B., 13, Indiana

What It Was Like: Trying Out for Football

When trying out for sports, especially football, girls need to stay calm and not get intimidated. Even though football is not thought of as a "girl's sport," a girl can do even better than a guy can. If the coaches try to discourage girls from trying out, do not give up—not even if girls need to get their parents involved. Also, always do your very best. As unfair as it may sound, what may be an average football tryout for a guy might seem mediocre to a doubtful coach if a girl gave such a performance.

Also, girls shouldn't take any disrespect from the guys trying out or who are already on the team. As always, two wrongs don't make a right, but no girl should have to stand for rude, sexist comments. Just remember to keep your head on straight and have confidence in yourself.

—Ashley W., 13, Maryland

Specific Sports Tips

Want to succeed at tennis? Practice. Do the drills. Train hard every day or three times a week. Listen to your coach. Set high goals for yourself, but don't forget to have fun.

—Melissa C., USA

Cross country really let me get my feelings out. If I was stressed, I could just run away and still do something positive. I recommend the sport to everyone.

—Adrianna M., USA

It Happened to Me

What's your tryout story? Write what it was like to try-out for a sport here. If you haven't tried out yet, make up what you'd like to have happen.

Want to win at volleyball? Practice your power serve! A good serve can often make the difference between winning and losing that game.

—Stephanie M.

For tennis, you need to practice; learn how to be very, very precise; and work hard on your skills. But it's a great sport to play. It encourages you to do and be your best.

—Zonia S.

> **WEBwatch**
>
> **COOL NURSE**
> Find out the best way to protect yourself from sports injuries. There are also cool articles on staying fit and keeping in shape.
>
> www.coolnurse.com/exercise_inj.htm

Field hockey teaches you teamwork and how to keep your cool under pressure. Winning is also really, really cool because then comes the pizza party!

—Jamie G.

I don't want to brag, but being team captain of our hockey team was soooo cool. Really helping to shore up defense and help newer players makes me feel good inside. There's lots of room for improvement, but next year we'll do even better.

—Rosa M.

When you're doing really well in soccer, don't let it go to your head. That can hurt how you play.

—Nikki E.

Don't forget about warming up and stretching, and drink lots of water before, during, and after you play. If you get tired or hurt, stop. Learn to take good care of your body. Then your body will do its best for you.

—Shareeka L.

Being Your Best at Home

Vacation Time Is Boring! What's the Best Way to Have More Fun?

The Problem Dear Being Your Best: Throughout the summer and winter vacations, I don't know what to do with my life! I know that might sound a little silly, but the problem is I've run out of ideas for what to do with my time—other than watch some rerun on TV or do homework. Do you have any suggestions?

— Nicky, 15, USA

A Solution Dear Nicky: You're in luck 'cause I've got tons! Below are 30 great ways to spend your time. Here's all you need to do: Get a pen or pencil and go down the list below, checking off the things that sound appealing.

When you're done, if you are on the Internet, surf www.askjeeves.com, and ask a question on a particular subject with an instant search engine response.

After your Internet browsing, you should have a pretty good idea about what interests you. From the ideas listed here, create your own personalized list, and make time to do things daily. Most of all, have fun!

1. Join a local club, such as drama, art, magic, debate, or poetry.
2. Try out for a sports team in your area.
3. Take up a musical instrument, such as the violin, guitar, or piano.
4. Volunteer your time at a hospital, retirement home, or animal shelter.
5. Volunteer to become a tutor for younger kids.
6. Take part in a fundraising effort for an important cause.
7. Start a school/class newspaper at your high school. If one already exists, try out for the staff.
8. Sign up for races in your area—5K or 10K runs, for example.
9. Look for a small, part-time job—anything from babysitting to shop clerk to receptionist.
10. Take up quilting or knitting, and use several of your finished projects as gifts during the holidays.
11. Start a collection of something fun—such as stamps, antiques, coins—and take pride in organizing and displaying it.
12. Look up casting calls in your area for theater, and try out for some productions.
13. Help your mom cook dinner. Look up new recipes or buy some cookbooks and help serve original, fresh dinners.
14. Start your own club with a bunch of friends who share your interests. Make a newsletter, schedule club meetings, and have fun!
15. Sign up for language courses at your local community college.
16. Help organize a block party in your neighborhood.

17. Throw a surprise party for your best friend.
18. Write about your experiences in a journal.
19. Design a Web page on something important, such as an environmental problem. (Editor's note: you can publish it on A Girl's World!)
20. Build a fort in your backyard for your younger siblings (if you have any).
21. Look for enrichment classes in your area, such as yoga, painting, political philosophy, tennis, or journalizing, and sign up!
22. Buy a bike, learn to ride (if you haven't already), and use your free time to ride around your neighborhood.
23. Download music on the Internet, and listen to the great tunes blasting from your speakers.
24. Arrange dates with your mom or dad so you can spend time with them; go out to dinner, to a concert, or to a sporting event.
25. Write a letter to the editor of your local newspaper or a national magazine on something you find important.
26. Look up the name of your favorite author on the Web and get info on new books coming out, or read entire novels of theirs online! (Hint: Try Orson Scott Card or Madeleine L'Engle.)

TAKE A TRIP TO ANOTHER COUNTRY BY STAYING AT HOME!

Pick a country from a map that you don't know anything about. Then go to the library and find a cookbook. Read about the country, then get your whole family together to cook a meal from that place. Add in a movie or some music, and you have one of the best family nights ever!

27. Take your best friend to a theme park or gaming area (ice-skating, bowling, etc.).
28. Sign up as an editor or advice columnist for A Girl's World Online!
29. Spend your free time writing short stories or poetry, and submit them to a teen magazine, to a contest, or to Girl's World.
30. Research something that interests you at the library or on the Web, such as famous actresses, euthanasia, global warming, feminism in the twenty-first century, etc.

— Melody, 13, California

What's the Best Way to Share a Room?

The Problem You have no privacy. You clean the room and your sister messes it UP. Or your sister is a clean freak and you're not. Her friends are always there. She uses your things without asking. She hates your kind of music and won't let you listen to the songs you like. She overhears your phone conversations and teases you about them.

A Solution How you feel about sharing a room depends on a lot.

Areas of Conflict:
- your interests
- respect for each other's things
- differences in ages

- study habits
- bedtimes
- favorite music
- television-watching habits
- types of friends you have
- how neat or messy you each are

First, consider the good things about sharing. If you are scared or upset, your sister is right there to comfort you. If she's a little older, she can give you advice about things that haven't happened to you yet. You'll never have to be lonely. But if you are living your life in anger and your relationship is getting worse, it's time to bring your feelings into the open in a positive and organized way.

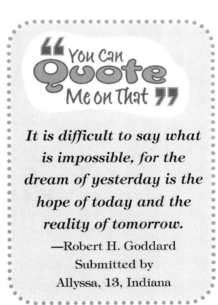

It is difficult to say what is impossible, for the dream of yesterday is the hope of today and the reality of tomorrow.
—Robert H. Goddard
Submitted by
Allyssa, 13, Indiana

Plan of Action . . .

1. *Write down your feelings.* Make one list of what bothers you and one of what's okay about living together (or is even good). In a quiet time, ask your sister (or roomie) to make the same kind of lists. Sit down and exchange lists. Read them carefully.

2. *Now, don't attack; talk.* Discuss what hurts, what's embarrassing, what is uncomfortable, and what's driving you nuts. Pick one item from her list and one item on your list that means neither of you can live peacefully unless there's a change here. Work on just that one item from each list. Try to find a way to reach a compromise.

Q. My family and friends think I'm a black sheep. If anything goes wrong, the first one they accuse is me. I keep trying to argue, but they won't listen. What can I do?

—Jessica, 13, Malaysia

1 Speak up strongly. Tell everyone that it's not fair to blame everything on you. You aren't responsible, and you won't take it anymore!

Mostly disagree   Somewhat disagree   Somewhat agree   Mostly agree

2 There must be a family member who knows you aren't always to blame (maybe an aunt, uncle, grandparent?). Get that person on your side and have them talk to the rest of the family.

Mostly disagree   Somewhat disagree   Somewhat agree   Mostly agree

3 Find out who really did whatever it is they are accusing you of and prove that they did it, not you.

Mostly disagree   Somewhat disagree   Somewhat agree   Mostly agree

4 Beat them to the punch. The next time you see a family member doing something bad, go immediately and tell your parents so they won't have time to blame you.

Mostly disagree   Somewhat disagree   Somewhat agree   Mostly agree

5 Don't pay any attention to the accusations. Just ignore them. You know you didn't do it, and that's what counts.

Mostly disagree   Somewhat disagree   Somewhat agree   Mostly agree

3. *Redecorate your room.* If your parents agree, think of new ways to decorate your shared room in a half-and-half style; what you *like* on your side. Or compromise. She can have that Jonathan Taylor poster up, and you get your picture of Alanis Morissette. You can even get a screen or curtain room divider if you want more privacy. Think about having separate shelves, if that's practical.

4. *Use earphones on your CD player or TV if you can.* You can boogie to your kind of music or program without driving her nuts, and vice versa. This also applies to playing music while your roomie is studying or sleeping.

5. *Respect each other.* This means that if you borrow anything, you must ask first. Don't just take your sister's new blouse. If she sees you wearing it, you may be looking at a big fight. Your sister needs to respect your stuff, too. Encourage her to ask you when she wants to borrow something. Learn to be careful with each other's stuff. If you break or damage something, offer to repair or replace it immediately. This is only polite. If this doesn't work, or you have problems remembering which clothing belongs to whom, another choice is to label everything "mine" and "yours" and respect the labels.

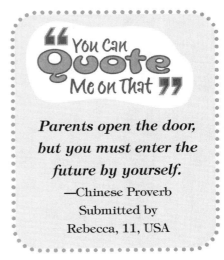

Parents open the door, but you must enter the future by yourself.
—Chinese Proverb
Submitted by
Rebecca, 11, USA

—Written with advice from Lynn, Gina, Angela, and Karen

Journalize It!

Tell It!

Dear Journal:

This is what I'd really like to tell my brother or sister right now . . .

Q. My parents are trying to stop smoking, and it's really hard for them. Do you have any suggestions for what I can do to help?

— Darleen, 14, North Dakota

1 First, I'd make sure that there is no temptation. If any of your relatives or their friends come into the house smoking, politely take them aside and ask them not to smoke around your parents.

Mostly disagree   Somewhat disagree   Somewhat agree   Mostly agree

2 Just don't bring it up. Talking about it with them will just make them want a cigarette more.

Mostly disagree   Somewhat disagree   Somewhat agree   Mostly agree

3 Find some great books or pamphlets on quitting smoking and bring them home for your folks.

Mostly disagree   Somewhat disagree   Somewhat agree   Mostly agree

4 Just encourage them to hang in there and stick with it. Tell them you are proud of them for trying so hard.

Mostly disagree   Somewhat disagree   Somewhat agree   Mostly agree

5 Turn into the anti-puff police! Case the house and make sure they haven't hidden any cigs. If so, get rid of them.

Mostly disagree   Somewhat disagree   Somewhat agree   Mostly agree

What's the Best Way to Borrow or Lend Money?

If your friends are always asking to borrow a buck, or you never have quite enough money and find yourself borrowing from them, here are some simple rules that can help you avoid arguments and save your friendships.

Borrowing Money

• Make borrowing a last resort. First, check that old piggy bank, have a garage sale, or try babysitting or other ways of making cash.

• Only borrow when it's an emergency. Little loans add up fast and are easy to forget.

• Be sure to tell your friends when you are going to repay them. Then do it when you said you would.

• If you borrow money, write yourself a reminder note on your calendar at home about when you are planning to pay back the loan. Then do it. Be sure to pay your friend back without having to be asked. That's important.

COMICS
Everyone loves a laugh, and this is a perfect site to find those perfect comics.
www.comics.com/

• Be prepared to pay back your loan soon. And don't borrow money you can't afford to repay at your next allowance.

• If you promised to pay a loan back by a certain date and you can't do it, don't just hope your friend will forget. Be responsible. Go to them and explain your problem.

- Don't make a habit of borrowing from everyone. No one wants a friend who is a constant "moocher."

Lending Money

- If you loan money out and expect to be repaid, be sure to tell your friend that. Say, "Here, I'm loaning you five dollars. Think you can get it back to me by next Saturday? I'm really going to need it then."

- Do you lend other kids money all the time? Be sure to keep a list. Write down who you loaned money to, how much it was, and when. That way, you won't mix loans up.

- Don't ever charge interest. You're a friend, not a bank.

- If you have a friend who borrows money from you and never repays you unless you bug her for it, don't loan her money. Just say no. It's too much wear and tear on your friendship if she won't pay you back without your begging her.

- Don't quibble over quarters. If your friend is 25 cents short on a movie ticket and you can help out, don't expect to be paid back. The idea is that your friend will help you the next time you are a quarter short.

- If you just can't or really don't want to make a loan, be nice. "I'd really like to help you out, but I just can't right now."

- Don't loan money you can't afford to lose.

- If someone owes you money and you need it back, remind them gently. "You probably just forgot, but I could really use that five dollars you borrowed a couple of weeks ago."

- Don't get a reputation for always loaning money to everyone. Some kids will take advantage of your generosity.

—Written with advice from Lynn, Gina, Angela, and Karen

Q. My parents are getting divorced, and now they're fighting about who is going to keep my brother and me. I would prefer to stay with my mom because my dad gets really busy and sometimes only gets home after ten o'clock. How should I tell him this without hurting his feelings?

— Carrie, 14, Arizona

1 Just tell your dad that you love him, but he's so busy, you'd be lonely living with him.

Mostly disagree   Somewhat disagree   Somewhat agree   Mostly agree

2 Tell your mom how you feel, and ask her to tell him.

Mostly disagree   Somewhat disagree   Somewhat agree   Mostly agree

3 Just try living with him. Having some time to yourself can be really great.

Mostly disagree   Somewhat disagree   Somewhat agree   Mostly agree

4 Tell your dad that you'll come to live with him but only if he gets home earlier.

Mostly disagree   Somewhat disagree   Somewhat agree   Mostly agree

5 Tell your dad that because you are a girl, you would feel more comfortable living with mom—in your teen years especially.

Mostly disagree   Somewhat disagree   Somewhat agree   Mostly agree

What's the Best Way to Deal When Your Brother Is Autistic?

The Problem Dear Being Your Best: I've got a little brother who is autistic, which means my mom has to spend heaps of time with him. I can't go and stay with my dad because my mom needs me to help with my brother, and my dad is always moving because of his job.

I'm getting to an age where I want to spend time with my mom and ask her some questions and things. But she spends so much time with my brother! I can't have friends around a lot either because they make fun of him, my mom says no, or my brother wrecks it. I know it's not his fault that there's something wrong with him. I love him very much, but sometimes it's really hard on me. My mom doesn't seem to understand that. What should I do?

Sign me,

—Sad, 12, USA

A Solution Dear Sad: I'm not able to tell you that I understand what you're going through because I don't, so that would be a lie. But I do have a few suggestions that I think may be able to help you out.

To my understanding, you appear to be feeling a little left out and like you have no social life. While you love your little brother a lot and don't mind helping your mum care for him, you still need to have some time to yourself and some quality time with your mother. I have come up with a few ideas that you may be able to try. I hope things work out for you.

1. Talk to your mum, tell her that you would like to spend some time with her without your little brother tagging along.

Maybe you have some relatives (aunts, uncles, grandparents) or a family friend who wouldn't mind caring for your brother for an afternoon each week while you and your mum can have some "girls time." Whether you go to a movie, do some shopping, or just hang about at home and play board games or have a chat is up to you, but at least then you'd be getting the time with your mum that you need. If none of your relatives are prepared to commit themselves to watching your brother once a week, then maybe you could opt for a less frequent time slot, such as once a fortnight or even once a month. If this plan falls through, then check out my next idea!

2. If you can't get my first idea up and running, then maybe you should go for something that doesn't require anyone else's cooperation apart from yours and your mother's. Maybe you could set aside a certain time each evening for you two to just talk. You could just tell her about what you're doing at school, show her some of your work, or ask her questions about things you might be worried about. It might be for only a half hour or maybe less, but you'd still be having your mother/daughter time, and that is what counts. The best time would probably be when your brother is taking a nap, or if he doesn't take naps, perhaps you could do it after he has been put to bed so he won't be up and about to disturb you.

3. Whatever idea you try, one thing is certain. You need to sit down and talk to everyone so they know how you feel! When you have friends over, make sure your mum knows that you would like her to keep your brother out of your way. Talk to her, okay? She won't bite your head off for wanting a little privacy!

4. If your friends come over and say things about your little brother, then are they really your friends? True friends wouldn't criticize your family for something that is beyond their control. So tell your friends that you don't like the way they treat him.

And if they continue to be nasty, then you're better off without them!

Well, Sista-gal, that's it from me. . . . Keep your chin up and smile! You're one brave and unselfish girl, but sometimes you do need to put yourself first, OK?! Just get out there and do what your heart tells you, and remember we all love you!

—Karissa P., 13, Australia

What's the Best Way to Deal When Siblings Tease?

The Problem Dear Being Your Best: I need help. My brother and sister always say that I am fat and ugly. They make me feel bad. I can't change who I am. What do I do?

Sign me,

—Need Help!, 12, USA

A Solution Dear Need Help: I know how you're feeling! I used to have this very same problem with my brothers. I know how awful they can make you feel, and it can really destroy your self-confidence, but (as hard as this may seem) DON'T WORRY about them!

The thing you need to have clear in your mind is whether YOU are happy with yourself. YOU are YOU, and that's what makes you so special. The world would be so boring if everybody was the way your brother and sister wanted the world to be, wouldn't it? So be proud of who you are! The key here is not to take the things they say to heart because chances are they are

Q. I have this problem, and it's a family issue. I have two stepbrothers. I think the younger one likes me, and it feels really awkward to be with him sometimes. What do you think I should do?

—Jessica, 13, West Virginia

1 As long as you just "think" he likes you, just don't encourage him.

Mostly disagree   Somewhat disagree   Somewhat agree   Mostly agree

2 Tell your mom that you think he has a crush on you, and ask her how to handle it.

Mostly disagree   Somewhat disagree   Somewhat agree   Mostly agree

3 Talk to him directly and say you like him but not "that" way. It isn't appropriate, since you are living in the same house.

Mostly disagree   Somewhat disagree   Somewhat agree   Mostly agree

4 Just bring home a boyfriend (or guy who is a friend) and give him the hint that you are already taken.

Mostly disagree   Somewhat disagree   Somewhat agree   Mostly agree

5 Just pretend you don't have a clue how he feels. He'll grow out of it.

Mostly disagree   Somewhat disagree   Somewhat agree   Mostly agree

only joking and doing it to get a reaction from you. It may be difficult to get them to stop, particularly if you are getting upset over what they are saying. But if you stop giving them the satisfaction of teasing you, then they will stop. The question is, how do you stop giving them the satisfaction of upsetting you, right? Check this out!

- PLAN A: Pretend it doesn't bother you when they call you names. Thank them for their input, and then tell them that you really don't care what they think. This works on the same principles I have mentioned above . . . if they don't see that you're upset, then they won't feel the need to continue teasing you. Give it a try . . . if it doesn't work, then try Plan B!

- PLAN B: Point out to them that everyone has faults, even them. Maybe name a few of theirs—but don't be too awful to them, or you'll be giving them the motivation they need to keep teasing you! Tell them that if they were to walk around treating everyone the way they treat you, they'd have no friends. Tell them that no one is perfect, especially not them because perfect people don't tease others. Ask them why they are paying so much attention to you! Otherwise move on to plan C!

- PLAN C: If it can't be solved between yourselves, you may need to bring in higher powers!! Talk to your mum or dad about it. Tell them what your brother and sister are saying to

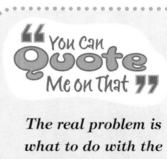

The real problem is what to do with the problem-solvers after the problems are solved.

—Gay Talese
Submitted by
Tessa, 16, Maryland

Journalize It!

Secret Problems

What problems do you hide from your family? Write about them—either below or on a separate sheet of paper.

you and how it makes you feel. Maybe they could have a word on your behalf? This is the final thing you can do. If your siblings won't let up after being spoken to by your parents, then they obviously don't respect themselves enough!

GOOD LUCK! And always remember, Sista... You are what you think you are, and you are soooooooo beautiful. Don't let anyone tell you otherwise, OK? Keep smiling!!!!! :-)

—Karissa P., 13, Australia

What's the Best Way to Deal When Friends Make Fun of Your Mom?

The Problem Dear Being Your Best: My mom has been sick with a disease for over seven years. All my friends go out all the time and wonder why I don't. They make fun of me and my mom. What should I do?

—Haley, 10, USA

A Solution Dear Haley: If these people are really your friends, they probably wouldn't be making fun of you or your mom. If you think they truly are your friends, telling them that it really bothers you when they say stuff like that ought to get them to lay off you and your mom.

The thing about friends is sometimes they're not mind readers. If they don't know it bothers you, they might just be doing it to keep the teasers from changing subjects to them! I've done it myself.

142 Chapter 6

Q. My brother, who is really nice to me, moved to college far away. I miss him so much. What do you suggest I do?

—Laura, 10, Florida

1 You can always set up a time to chat online with him.

Mostly disagree   Somewhat disagree   Somewhat agree   Mostly agree

2 You'll just have to realize that he's a lot older and he's growing up. He won't be spending as much time with his family.

Mostly disagree   Somewhat disagree   Somewhat agree   Mostly agree

3 Just send him e-mail letters that tell him how you feel. Hopefully, you two can start a regular correspondence.

Mostly disagree   Somewhat disagree   Somewhat agree   Mostly agree

4 Phone him once a week at a prearranged time.

Mostly disagree   Somewhat disagree   Somewhat agree   Mostly agree

5 Try to get closer to friends your age so that you'll be too busy to miss him a lot.

Mostly disagree   Somewhat disagree   Somewhat agree   Mostly agree

When a parent is sick, it's hard on you, too. It's hard because your mom can't help being sick, and you can't help it either. So tell your friends exactly whazzup with your mom. Don't be afraid to talk about her illness. You need support from your friends. They can't give it unless they know what's going on.

When they make fun of you, stand up for yourself. Tell them that it bothers you. If these people are really your friends, they wouldn't intentionally hurt your feelings.

If telling them to stop doesn't work, you might want to consider getting new friends. You don't have to put up with being insulted. No one does. No one should put up with that kind of treatment. Why? Because it sends a message to people that it's okay to say that kind of thing. And it's not.

Don't be afraid to go to your school counselor to talk. You shouldn't have to face this kind of peer pressure alone.

—Avrila K., 13, Oregon

What's the Best Way to Buy a Gift for Your Guy?

The Problem Dear Being Your Best: My boyfriend's birthday is in a couple of days, and I don't know what to give him. Please, help me!

—Clara, 12, USA

A Solution Dear Clara: I have a boyfriend, too, and I know exactly what you're going through! Picking out a present for a guy at a younger age is really tough! But there are a lot of things you can do.

Q. Whenever my mom and I have a disagreement, like about my going to my friend's house or something, I try to talk about it with her and let her see my point of view. But Mom never listens to me and ends up screaming at the top of her lungs. How can I get her to CALMLY talk about things?

— Hannah, 14, California

1 I'd make sure you don't ask her to do something when she's already upset about something else. Make sure she's calm before you ask her.

Mostly disagree   Somewhat disagree   Somewhat agree   Mostly agree

2 Wait for a quiet time, then talk to your mom in general about why you two are always in screaming matches and what can you do to make things easier.

Mostly disagree   Somewhat disagree   Somewhat agree   Mostly agree

3 Tell your mom you love her, but can she loosen up by letting you do simple things like visiting a friend?

Mostly disagree   Somewhat disagree   Somewhat agree   Mostly agree

4 If she screams at you, don't scream back. It just makes things worse.

Mostly disagree   Somewhat disagree   Somewhat agree   Mostly agree

5 Your mom may have some serious problems on her mind. Before an argument starts, just ask her how she is, and if something is bothering her, would she like to talk about it with you?

Mostly disagree   Somewhat disagree   Somewhat agree   Mostly agree

1. Find out more about him. What's his favorite sport, color, activity, or just about anything else. When you know what he likes, it might be easier to pick something out.

2. Try the direct approach: Go right up to him and ask: "So, what do you want for your birthday?"

3. Do you know any boys that are just friends? I sure do. This is how I usually get my boyfriend presents. If you have a boy that's a friend, maybe he's also friends with your boyfriend! If so, ask him what he might want for his birthday or what he likes.

Shopping Tips

- When picking out a present for a guy at an age like ours, try to stay in budget. I would say spend no more than maybe about $15.00 at the most on him. I mean, think. If you spend millions of dollars on him and get him a GREAT present, he's probably gonna feel pretty guilty that you did so much for him.

- Do NOT give him money if you can't find him something. Believe me, I got money from my boyfriend once. I would have much rather gotten a present he picked out, or even a late birthday present if it had to be. I also felt really guilty with the money.

- Think about the problem as if you were your boyfriend. What does he do for fun, where might he go shopping? Obviously not the women's department!

- Go to guy stores—maybe a baseball card shop or something like that. I mean, he'd probably be pretty disappointed if you bought him some nail polish!

If Nothing Works . . .

If none of the above helps, ask your friends for help. Or even your boyfriend because if there's anyone who knows more about him, it's your boyfriend himself.

Well, Clara, I hope I helped you solve your problem! Much love,

—Caroline H., USA

What's the Best Way to Get and Keep Your First Job?

The Problem Dear Being Your Best: How do you get and keep your first job?

—Terri, 14, Oregon

A Solution Dear Terri: Here's some tips on how to get that first job.

1. *Think about your goals.* How much time do you have to work? Ten hours a week? The goal is to earn some money, get some experience, but *not* to stumble through the rest of your life. Here's some warning signs that your job is too demanding: Your grades begin to fall. Your friends and family barely recognize you. Your pet doesn't know you. Chances are, you're working too much. Make it a priority to find a work schedule that works for you. Schedule time for study, time for fun, and time to hang out with family and friends.

2. *Make decisions.* Which is more important to you: earning money, or getting experience and contacts in a field you love? In ten years, do you see yourself working with animals? Or as a doctor? Or in the fashion industry? Look around for part-time jobs that will give you a taste of the future.

3. *Get ready to work.* Get a social security card. Go to the phone book and find the number for the social security office. Call them. In most states, they'll mail you an application. You'll need a copy of your birth certificate and a school ID card.

4. *Find out about the laws that regulate work for girls your age.* The Federal Fair Labor Standards Act protects you from employers who might pay you too little or ask you to do work that is dangerous. Contact your local Employment Development office for this information. Be informed.

5. *Have the paperwork ready.* Do you need special papers from school in order to work? Check with your school's guidance office. Impress future employers by having all your paperwork together and ready to go.

Finding That First Job

Ask everyone you know: your friends, their parents, your teachers, your parents' friends. Sit down and talk with them. Tell them you're looking for a job. Tell them what your interests are. Connections are the most common way everyone finds out about jobs.

Go to your school guidance office, your local library; check your phone book, your state employment service. Don't forget to check the newspaper every day. Look for "Help Wanted" signs. Go to the places you'd like to work.

Here are some ideas:

- vet's office
- dog/animal boarding care facilities
- stables
- daycare centers
- clothing stores
- parks and recreation departments
- pools
- beaches

- supermarkets
- theatres
- schools

Handling Your First Interview

- Dress for success. Look good, clean, neat. Wear nice shoes. Be sure you have a good haircut.
- Everybody knows this one, but here is just a reminder: Don't chew gum.
- Don't bring your friends or your phone. Bring yourself and a smile.
- Show up early so you can fill out the paperwork.
- Leave enough time to go to the bathroom and spruce up. Comb your hair. Wash your hands with warm water so you're not so shaky.
- Be nice to everyone you meet. If you work there, you'll have to get along with everyone, from the delivery girl to the president.
- Bring your social security card and some letters of recommendation from teachers or your soccer coach or your church.
- Have a good reason why you want to work there.
- Tell them why they should hire you: You're a hard worker. You're good with people. You finish jobs. You're a self-starter. Think about what's good about you and tell them. Don't wait for them to ask. You ran the school bake sale? Tell them all the jobs you did.
- Be interesting and interested. If you're bored by going in looking for a job, they'll be bored, too. If you smile, have some energy, seem interested; they'll catch the mood.
- Be ready to tell them how you plan to get to and from work. Not everyone has access to a car.

- Look at the interviewers when you talk to them. Make eye contact.

- Don't be afraid to ask questions: What will be expected of you on this job? Are there any chances for advancement?

- Play on your strengths. You don't have a lot of work experience (maybe not any!), but you've had chances to lead, run things, be responsible. Talk about what you can bring to a job besides a warm body.

- Don't squirm, pick your nails, or fidget. Yes, you're nervous. Show you can handle stress by being calm, cool, and collected.

- You're starting at the bottom. It's okay. Let them know that you're willing to learn their business and work your way up.

- After the interview, send a thank-you note to the person you talked to. It's customary.

The First Day at Work

- Get lots of rest.
- Eat breakfast.
- Do your best to look and feel great.
- Get there early.
- Have everything you need with you—all the papers.
- Don't be surprised if you have to fill out more papers. That's the way things are.
- Try to remember everyone's name.
- Take notes on what is expected of you.
- Listen more than you talk.
- If your fellow employees are complaining, don't join in.

Q. I'm 13, and some say I act like a 20-year-old. My problem is that my sister (age 14) and my cousin (13 1/2) act like a pair of 2-year-olds. If I don't take responsibility, who will? My sis and cousin tell me I don't know how to have fun, but I do. I know when it's a time to play and when to take things seriously. What would you do?

—Julie, 13, California

1 If your cousin and sis want to act immature, let them. Just do your own thing, and don't feel responsible for them.

Mostly disagree   Somewhat disagree   Somewhat agree   Mostly agree

2 You should never change to please someone else. You say you know when to have fun, so when it's a "fun" time, invite your cousin and sis along so they'll see you in "play" mode.

Mostly disagree   Somewhat disagree   Somewhat agree   Mostly agree

3 Maybe what you consider to be "fun," they don't. Find friends whose interests better match your own.

Mostly disagree   Somewhat disagree   Somewhat agree   Mostly agree

4 Just leave your cuz and sis alone. You are growing up faster than they are. Just wait and they'll catch up.

Mostly disagree   Somewhat disagree   Somewhat agree   Mostly agree

5 Examine your life. Is it really true that you never have much fun and take things too seriously? If you find that it's true, loosen up a bit.

Mostly disagree   Somewhat disagree   Somewhat agree   Mostly agree

- You're going to make mistakes. It's part of learning. Just smile and keep going. Try not to make the same mistake twice.

Surviving the Job

- Phone if you're going to be late.
- Only call in sick if you're really sick. People are depending on you.
- Talk directly to your boss or supervisor. Messages left with the gang at work can get garbled.
- Do the best job you can.
- Don't try to be Wonder Woman and burn yourself out completely the first week.
- f you absolutely hate the work, hate the people, hate everything about the job, give your boss two weeks' notice and quit. You found this job; you can find others.

—Davina, 16, California

What's the Best Way to Throw a Party?

First, make a list of all the people you're going to invite. Then make up the invitations and send them to the people at least a week before the party (just so they can have it planned). I would have lots of food and ask around what kind my guests would like. If you have to have someone looking after the party, I strongly suggest that you ask an older brother or a sister, rather than a parent.

Try to invite an even number of boys and girls. If you want to have a party people will be talking about, have music that they like. Try not to put too many slow songs on, but wait until kids ask for slow songs. Keep it lively, or your guests will start to get bored.

During the party, try to make sure that not too many people are sitting alone on the sidelines. Try to say hi to everyone who is there so no one thinks you are trying to avoid them.

— D.J., 13, Canada

Have a Polaroid camera by the door, and as you welcome your guests, snap their picture. Use this for your scrapbook or as a parting gift to your guest.

— Lois, Mississippi

STRANGE BUT FUN
Here's something totally strange but fun. It's a site that has the history of Band-Aids, all the ads, the canisters, fun stuff. Check it out and then start your own collection.
www.savetz.com/bandaid/

If it is a co-ed (boy-girl) party and you want couples, make as many couples as you can. If the other people who aren't paired with anyone have boyfriends/girlfriends who go to different schools, tell them to let their boyfriend or girlfriend come. Or if you know someone who could be paired with a person who goes to another school, invite them!

— Jessica, 12, Alabama

Being the Best Person You Can Be

What's the Best Way to Start at a New School?

The Problem Dear Being Your Best: Last year I started at a new school. I was shy at first, and I really did not want to go. So . . . I threw fits and acted really immature. I did not like anyone because I wanted to go to my old school. But soon I realized that no one liked me because I was acting like a brat. So I told every one I was sorry, and now I have a lot of new friends!

—Andi C., Michigan

A Solution Dear Andi: Thanks for sharing your experiences. Going to a new school is really hard. But here's some survival tips that might make it easier next time.

- See if you can check out the school before it opens. If they have an orientation, go to it. Find out where everything

How Do You Feel Rich?

The funny thing about it is that being rich and feeling rich can be two different things. Some people who have little feel as though they're blessed with everything they want. Some people feel there's never enough, no matter what they have. Some people have great friends and feel like that makes them the richest people on earth. Think of all the blessings you have that make you feel rich. Then make a collage here (use cutouts from magazines or pictures that represent the items on your list). Now show off your wealth to a friend. You go, girl!

is, like your classes and the bathrooms. That way you won't have to be asking everyone and feel silly.

- Break the ice. Be the first to introduce yourself. Try to remember the other kids' names. Start conversations. Ask the kids about themselves, such as what they like.

- Smile. Don't be in a rush to make friends. Get to know everyone first.

- Don't forget why you're there: to learn. Stay on top of your schoolwork and homework.

- Don't let the blues overtake you. Get involved. Join some clubs or activities.

- Don't forget your old friends. Write them. Stay in touch.

—Jennie, 12, USA

Fear less, hope more;
Complain less,
breathe more;
Talk less, say more;
Hate less, love more;
And all good things
are yours.

—Swedish Proverb
Submitted by
Melanie, 15, Texas

What's the Best Way to Be Both Smart and Cool?

The Problem Dear Being Your Best: I am normally a straight-A student, and I still am. This year I am going into the

Q. My school life is being ruined by a loud-mouthed girl who is the "best" at everything. Not only do the kids in class worship her, but the teacher also pays more attention to her than anyone else. What can I do to get some attention from my teacher?

—Bridget, 10, Louisiana

1 You should talk to your teacher after class. Tell him or her that you have something to contribute, too, and that he or she should call on you and not just this girl all the time.

   Mostly disagree   Somewhat disagree   Somewhat agree   Mostly agree

2 Talk to your parents and ask them to talk to the teacher about the problem. This girl shouldn't be "hogging" all the teacher's attention.

   Mostly disagree   Somewhat disagree   Somewhat agree   Mostly agree

3 I'd talk to the girl directly. Ask her to back off and let the others in class answer some questions or participate more. She has no right to dominate the class.

   Mostly disagree   Somewhat disagree   Somewhat agree   Mostly agree

4 You should probably tell the school counselor about it and ask him or her what would be the best thing to do.

   Mostly disagree   Somewhat disagree   Somewhat agree   Mostly agree

5 I'd just get your parents to talk to her parents about it. Let them work it out for you.

   Mostly disagree   Somewhat disagree   Somewhat agree   Mostly agree

6th grade and might actually skip to the 7th. It is in discussion, but I am afraid that I will be made fun of like the other smart kids in my school. What can I do to fit in and prove I can be both smart and cool?

— Maria, 11, USA

A Solution Dear Maria: Well, it is possible to be smart and cool. You can be into the same music and do the same things for fun. Once kids see that they have a few things in common with you, they should be comfortable hanging with you.

These days it doesn't matter what people think about you or say about you as long as you are your own person. You have something that maybe some kids want, but don't let them use you because you're smart. Don't let anyone copy your homework or copy from you on tests. That's no way to make real friends.

Smart kids, like you, are very appreciated at my school, and, usually, smart kids make the best friends because they have the best answers to life's questions and they give great advice. Most of my friends are smart, and I don't treat them any differently, and people shouldn't treat you bad either. If they do, just remember who is going to have the career!!!

— Kim, 17, Canada

What's the Best Way to Deal with Being Bullied?

The Problem Dear Being Your Best: I don't know if it's because I'm shy, but I've always been the victim of other kids who

Give Yourself a Break

You push it too hard. You know you do. School, sports, friends. . . . Stop for a moment and take a deep breath. Now exhale, slowly. Make a list of ten things you'd like to do if you had time to slow down.

1
2
3
4
5
6
7
8
9
10

Everyone wants to be her or his best. Go do one of the things on your list. You also need to rest and take some time for yourself.

like to tease and bully. This is ruining my life. What's up with this, and how can I stop it?

—Anonymous, 14, USA

A Solution   Dear Anonymous: This article is for all those girls out there who have ever been bullied or have ever bullied others. Bullying is a situation nobody deserves to go through. This probably sounds strange, but the bully quite likely feels insecure and finds bullying others a simple form of entertainment and a way to make friends. People often try and make friends with bullies to avoid becoming the next target! Insecure people often turn into bullies because by putting others down and drawing attention to their bad points, they are making themselves feel superior and are making themselves feel better about their own flaws and imperfections.

Bullying is a horrible thing for anyone to go through, but what you must remember is that it's nothing personal. A bully's target can change from one day to the next for no particular reason. Some really nice people get bullied; some people often get bullied because they *are* so nice, although that doesn't seem to make much sense.

How Can You Put a Stop to It?

I know it is hard to stand up to a bully, but you have to tell someone if you are being bullied! If you try to tell someone and they don't listen or take any notice, you have to persist. Tell someone you trust, someone you can confide in. Speak to your parent, teacher, older brother or sister, auntie, nan, granddad, anyone!

INTERESTED IN OUR ENVIRONMENT?
Looking for a cool club to link up with? Check out Earth Team!
www.earthteam.net/

Preferably, tell your parents or another adult relative. If you don't normally talk to your parents about stuff like this, now is a good time to start!

"You Can Quote Me on That"

If you can DREAM it, you can DO it.
—Walt Disney
Submitted by Danasia, 14, USA

Your parents would probably be hurt if they knew you felt you couldn't talk to them about something so important, and they will probably be really helpful in this situation! Sit them down and tell them the situation, and listen to what they have to say! If you find that they don't have time or for some other reason aren't prepared to listen, then look for another adult in your family. No relative of yours is going to stand by and let you be bullied; therefore, it should get sorted out in no time at all.

Please speak out! Bullying is an awful thing and can often lead to suicide, depression, isolation, and lots of other unhappy situations! Just remember, you are helping everyone else as well, since the bully could turn on anyone, anytime, and make that person's life as miserable as your own! It can't really get much worse anyway, if you are so unhappy already.

Sticks and Stones May Break My Bones, but Words Will Never Hurt Me . . .
Words. Insults. Arguments. Rumors. These are often the most hurtful types of bullying. If someone hits you, it hurts for a few minutes—maybe a few days at the most—but insults and taunts and verbal abuse can leave a permanent wound. If someone calls you ugly, criticizes something you say or do, it will always be at the back of your mind and leave you wondering

whether it is really true. It may leave you emotionally damaged and can hurt you more than a broken leg!!

Insults and rumors are a form of bullying. Rumors are often very hurtful and can be extremely upsetting. Remember that if you are the target of a rumor, probably nobody actually believes these rumors, so don't worry about that!! People spread all sorts of rumors, even when they don't actually think they're true. They just pass on rumors so that they can appear popular, knowing all the latest gossip. Actually, they are bored and want something to talk about and to be in on the action and discuss what everyone else is talking about! People very rarely believe gossip, so don't worry! Wait for a little while, as these rumors will probably just blow over. After about a week, everyone will probably have forgotten all about you and be talking about something else! But if these rumors do not come to an end, you must tell someone and sort this out!

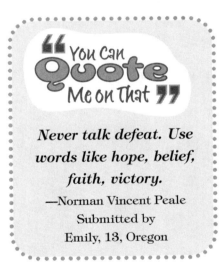

Never talk defeat. Use words like hope, belief, faith, victory.
—Norman Vincent Peale
Submitted by
Emily, 13, Oregon

How Would You Feel?

If you are reading this and you know that you have bullied people in the past, then just think about what you are doing. Just to make yourself feel or look bigger, you are wrecking people's lives! If you found out that one of your latest victims had just been found dead because you had led him or her to suicide, how would you feel? If you could see how unhappy that spotty girl in math was, how she went home in tears, how she believed herself ugly and worthless, how she woke up depressed and terrified of what would happen that day, just because of YOU, how

Chapter 7

The People in My Life Who Matter

Draw a picture here of your hero. It can be anyone who inspired you this week. Write a note to your hero next to the picture. Tell them why you appreciate who they are and what they do.

would you feel? Do you really have the right to ruin other peoples lives for the sake of your own enjoyment?

Put Yourself in the Bully Victim's Place
Imagine that yesterday you went to the optician's and discovered that your recent headaches were due to bad eyesight, so you were given glasses. Now all of your friends have decided that they don't want to talk to you or associate with you anymore because you are wearing glasses, and *everyone* is calling you "four eyes" and "geek." You have lost all your friends, and your life is being made miserable—just because your vision is a bit blurry when things are held close to you. Is this fair? Did you choose to have bad eyesight? Do you enjoy wearing glasses? Well, this is exactly what goes on in schools and other places; people are bullied for ridiculous reasons like this! Do you want to be responsible for causing so much pain to others? Are you being fair? If you think the answer to this is no, then why are you doing it?

I keep my ideals, because in spite of everything, I still believe that people are really good at heart.
—Anne Frank
Submitted by
Nikki, 12, California

One of the Gang!
People often skit (diss) others to fit in with their friends. If you think that by stopping bullying your friends won't respect you or want you in their gang, then think about what sort of friends they actually are! Would real "friends" stop liking you

Let It Be

Is there something in the past that is bothering you? Is there something you wish you could tell a friend, but you don't know who to tell? Write it down in this square.

Now use gel pens to write "Let It Be" all over the square until you can't read the words you wrote any longer. Then let what's troubling you go. Let it be. We hope you feel better doing this.

just because you aren't mistreating others like they are? Give them a chance, and they probably won't like you any less for it! If this is the case, though, and your "friends" don't want you around anymore, then you're probably best off without them! This may sound hard, but it is possible. Just start talking to people in your classes, join in with their conversations, join clubs, act confident, join in with people (even if you're not really that confident), and get to know people! Once people realize you're actually a nice person and you stop bullying, I guarantee you'll have a LOT more friends than before. You'll just have your old group of "friends" hating you, instead of the whole school!

You Can Do It!

Whether you are working up the courage to stand up to a bully and tell a teacher what is going on, or to go against your friends and stop bullying, then you will probably be apprehensive about it and full of doubts. Just remember: You can do anything you want! If you set your mind to it, you can achieve this and come through it a stronger and happier person! Good luck with everything!

—Julienne, 13, New York

Millions of kids are teased everyday. Especially girls. Now there is a site called Teasing Victims that can help you stop being a teasing victim in ten easy steps. You'll find ten lessons to learn and master.

Although it is a little difficult to remember to use the tricks, I found it very helpful. So check out the site and enjoy a more peaceful life. It even has tips on how to stop teasing if you are the one teasing.

Check out: Teasing Victims
www.teasingvictims.com

—Article by Shannon, 15, England

Q. My class went on the annual 6th grade camping trip, and my teacher (female) came along. We had to bring a male teacher 'cause of the rules, and now I think they like each other! What should my class and I do?

— Kathy, 11, Canada

1 If both are single, then just be glad for them. As long as they are both doing their jobs on the trip, just ignore it.

Mostly disagree   Somewhat disagree   Somewhat agree   Mostly agree

2 Hey, grown-ups get crushes, too. Maybe it will all blow over by the time you all return to school. So just leave them alone.

Mostly disagree   Somewhat disagree   Somewhat agree   Mostly agree

3 If they are ignoring their responsibilities to your class, then you should report it to the principal when you all return.

Mostly disagree   Somewhat disagree   Somewhat agree   Mostly agree

4 By "like," do you mean kissing in front of the kids? That isn't appropriate, and you should tell your parents.

Mostly disagree   Somewhat disagree   Somewhat agree   Mostly agree

5 Ask your female teacher if she likes this guy, and if they are both single, tell her to go for it. You support her.

Mostly disagree   Somewhat disagree   Somewhat agree   Mostly agree

Inspire Yourself

Feel run down? Run over? School, chores, all the usual problems your friends have can leave you feeling like it's all too much. Want to break out of the mold and feel inspired?

Try this: Get a pile of old magazines, the kind with lots of big glossy ads. Take a pair of scissors, then go through and cut out the words they use to sell some of the stuff you like. (It helps to have a big envelope to put them in.) Soon you'll have a pile of words like "beautiful," "great," "fresh," "powerful," and "spectacular."

Now get one of your favorite pictures of yourself (if you don't have a favorite picture, draw yourself as you would like to be) and put it here.

Glue the words you found around your picture. Don't forget words like "amazing" and "beautiful." Take a look at this page every day. Be inspired. Remember, you, too, are "spectacular" and "fabulous"!

What's the Best Way to Tame a Maxed-Out Schedule?

The Problem Dear Being Your Best: Hi! I'm 13 years old and actually have a really good life. Only thing is, I'm way too busy. During the year, I've got four to six days of ballet a week, piano every day, chorus once a week, and guitar once a week. I want to get into a really good high school, so I'm a straight-A student. I'm really worried about next year, that I'll have a nervous breakdown or something. What can I do? I don't want to quit anything, but the stress is really overwhelming. What's the best way to deal with this?

—Marianne, 13, USA

A Solution Dear Marianne: I am glad you are happy with your life, and that shows you must be happy with how you choose to spend your time. Obviously, you enjoy the activities you participate in, but you don't enjoy the way you are occupied every second of the day. I think you should take a deep breath and think calmly. If you are permanently worried about it, this will only add to your stress. Think if there is anything you would not mind giving up.

If there isn't anything, then you will just have to work around your activities. Make a chart, maybe in your diary, of the times

> **"You Can Quote Me on That"**
>
> *Honesty is the first chapter in the book of wisdom.*
> —Thomas Jefferson
> Submitted by
> Malika, 14, USA

you have your activities. Perhaps you could rearrange the times so they are not all close to each other. Then you would have a wide gap of free time. If you can't do this, then try spending the gaps in between your music and dancing classes doing your homework. Then after all your classes are finished, you will be able to spend the rest of your time doing whatever you want.

If you are still stressed and rushing around with no free time, then you should really reconsider the amount of activities you are doing. Do you really need to do ballet and piano that many times a week? If it is absolutely 100% necessary, then OK, but perhaps you could cut down a bit on the time you spend doing these things. If you are still really stressed with no free time, then you have to give something up. There is really no other option; your health is more important than dancing and music, and so is your social life. Heading toward a nervous breakdown is not going to help anyone. Even if you have to give something up now, you can always take it up later in life when you have more time on your hands.

Don't spend your time stressing about school either. It will only make you unhappy. Get out there and spend more time with your friends! After all, you are only young once. Make the most of it. And remember, worrying won't solve the situation. What happens will happen—with or without the worry!

—Shannon, 14, England

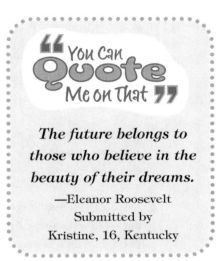

The future belongs to those who believe in the beauty of their dreams.
—Eleanor Roosevelt
Submitted by
Kristine, 16, Kentucky

Q. My friend has to bring in this permission slip saying she can come to a water park with our class. She keeps forgetting to bring it. If she doesn't bring it in, she can't go, and she wants to go. What should I do? Keep on reminding her?

— Nancy, 11, New York

1 Just remind her how much fun it will be and that you certainly expect her to be there.

Mostly disagree   Somewhat disagree   Somewhat agree   Mostly agree

2 Maybe she's not "forgetting." Maybe she's worried her folks will say no. Ask her if this is the problem. Let her confide in you.

Mostly disagree   Somewhat disagree   Somewhat agree   Mostly agree

3 Have your mom or dad call hers and say that you really want your friend on the trip with you. Have they signed the form yet?

Mostly disagree   Somewhat disagree   Somewhat agree   Mostly agree

4 Offer to take the form to her parents in case she's afraid to or worried about their reaction.

Mostly disagree   Somewhat disagree   Somewhat agree   Mostly agree

5 Just say, "Maybe you don't really want to go, or you would get the form signed." That should light a fire under her.

Mostly disagree   Somewhat disagree   Somewhat agree   Mostly agree

Being the Best Person You Can Be **171**

Q. My friend is 15, and she's having trouble with her mum. Her mum is 52, and she's got her nose, tongue, and eyelid pierced!! My friend is embarrassed. What should I do?

—Joanne, 10, United Kingdom

1 Tell your friend that her mom's "style" is just something she'll have to live with.

Mostly disagree   Somewhat disagree   Somewhat agree   Mostly agree

2 I'd talk to my friend's mom alone and tell her that her weird piercings are freaking out her daughter. Can she tone it down a bit?

Mostly disagree   Somewhat disagree   Somewhat agree   Mostly agree

3 Tell your friend that if she loves her mom, something like how she decorates her body shouldn't be an issue.

Mostly disagree   Somewhat disagree   Somewhat agree   Mostly agree

4 I would have your own mom talk to this woman and tell her that her actions are upsetting her daughter.

Mostly disagree   Somewhat disagree   Somewhat agree   Mostly agree

5 Tell this girl to get a life. Her mom is just being trendy.

Mostly disagree   Somewhat disagree   Somewhat agree   Mostly agree

What's the Best Way to Deal with Stress?

The Stress-Busters List
- Relax. Take breaks.
- Breathe. Stop and take deep breaths.
- Get lots of sleep.
- Eat good food.
- Get exercise.
- Accept what you can't change. The test is tomorrow? Deal.
- Watch your thoughts. If you're saying "could, would, should," change your thinking to "can, will, want to."
- Get organized.
- Manage your time.
- Don't compete 24 hours a day. Do your best, but don't always have to be the best.
- Be quiet once in a while.
- Be nice to yourself.
- Don't forget to have fun.

There are no great things, only small things with great love. Happy are those.
—Mother Teresa
Submitted by
Ruth, 11, Australia

More Stress-Buster Tips
Stress is as stress does. Huh? Stress is something all of us deal with. We feel it in family sadness, in abuse, and in hard homework. When we're older, it's teen anxiety, AP classes, boyfriend/friend relation-

ships, peer pressure, and major homework. We feel it in family problems, death, and hard days at school. But what can we do about it before it does something to us?

Stress can be a major problem that affects many people. It can cause illness and pain in severe cases and depression and unhappiness in other cases. Sometimes stress can be good, such as when we get adrenaline in a gymnastics competition or a race, but a lot of stress we could do without! Here's some things we can do about stress.

There are no shortcuts to any place worth going.
—Celine Dion
Submitted by
Clara, 11, Washington

1. Meditation and yoga. It may sound funny, but these relaxing techniques can help you come to grips with your feelings and let go of painful emotions.

2. Reflection at the end of the day about your day can also help release stress from your body, giving you a good sleep and a fresh mind when you wake up.

3. Often stress comes from family feuds and the so-called teenage rebellion issue. Although teenagers are expected to become independent human beings, it is not always necessary to get into fights about everything with your parents while defending yourself with the teenage rebellion factor. Face it, the world does not revolve around you. The sooner you realize this, the sooner you can mend it with your parents and just learn that you shouldn't question everything they say. Having a peaceful relationship with your parents can save you and your family a lot of trouble. If you're not a teen, it still pertains to you. Avoiding fights with your parents and your family makes life a whole lot easier.

Talk About

Q. Lately, my social life has gone downhill. I have stopped hanging out with friends, and people refer to me as "The Hermit" because I stay indoors 24/7. I don't do drugs, and I am still a good student. What should I do to help my problem?

— Heather, 14, USA

1 If you just like being alone to read or write or do solitary activities, there's nothing wrong with this. You don't have to be a social butterfly.

Mostly disagree   Somewhat disagree   Somewhat agree   Mostly agree

2 If you are depressed and that's why you are staying alone, then get medical help and counseling before it gets any worse.

Mostly disagree   Somewhat disagree   Somewhat agree   Mostly agree

3 If you used to hang with your friends a lot and now you don't, what changed in your life? If you haven't faced the change, maybe you need to confront it.

Mostly disagree   Somewhat disagree   Somewhat agree   Mostly agree

4 Why not ask a friend to come over and be a "hermit" with you for a weekend?

Mostly disagree   Somewhat disagree   Somewhat agree   Mostly agree

5 Maybe you are tired of your friends and need new ones. Try making friends who like some of the things you like to do.

Mostly disagree   Somewhat disagree   Somewhat agree   Mostly agree

4. If you're getting a lot of stress and peer pressure from your boyfriend or just your friends sometimes, you should take a time-out from a boyfriend-girlfriend relationship. When it's your friends, talk to a counselor or just your parents about life in general. Sometimes just talking can ease the frustration and pain, and lots of times others outside of the situation have good ideas to help you.

5. If a big test, school projects, or homework are major stressors, sometimes it's a good idea to find out why. You may just have a lot of homework, but other times it may be because you have too many extracurricular activities or are spending too much time with friends and getting behind. If that's the reason, then think about taking some time off your activities and allowing yourself more time to work on your homework and catch up.

6. Some people just get stressed from the buzz of everyday life. In today's world, things move fast, and sometimes you just need time, by yourself, to relax, take a good bubble bath, read a book, walk your dog, or just sleep!

7. Watching TV, I would say, doesn't really relieve stress; it's often just as fast-paced as regular life and quite loud as well. Computers aren't a great idea either when trying to relieve stress. Save your Internet time for later; your e-mail pals can wait.

8. If you're having a particularly stressful day, something nice to do is just go home, prepare yourself a steaming bubble bath, and slip in. Turn on some classical or alternative music—just don't fall asleep in the bath! After you get out of the tub, cook yourself something nice, like a chocolate dessert—no, now is not the time to go on an eating spree, just time to relax in the beauty and comfort of today's world. If chocolate sounds too sweet and too much of a cooking chore, make yourself some tea (decaf) to drink. If you want to relax on your bed for a while, that's fine, too.

Journalize It!

Feeling Good About Yourself

You know the key to a great relationship is to treat people how you'd like to be treated. So how would you like to be treated? Make a list here of ten ways people can show that they care about you and like you.

1
2
3
4
5
6
7
8
9
10

9. Meditation and yoga at this point might be fun to try, but don't neglect your homework. If you're having a particularly hard month, week, or whatever, try setting aside about an hour a day for yourself for relaxation purposes.

— Contributed by Melody D., USA

Stress happens when you get too mad and when everything is hard on you. So take away your stress. Do things like breathe in and breathe out. Make yourself calm. Have fun. That takes away all your stress.

— Monica M., USA

Do something for fun once in a while to get your mind off school. Just don't do anything you'll regret. I mean, go outside, shoot some hoops, walk around the park, whatever!

— Umbro

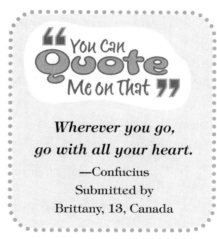

" You Can Quote Me On That "

Wherever you go, go with all your heart.
—Confucius
Submitted by
Brittany, 13, Canada

Here is one thing I do to keep myself relaxed and away from stress: Take things in stride and plan ahead! Especially the first couple of weeks of school. You're just trying to get back in the groove of things, and you don't need to get stressed out with all that homework, right?! For instance, you have a big game coming up on Wednesday, and you're just being piled up with homework. What do you do?

Well, the smart thing to do would be to calm down and don't get stressed. That doesn't help the matter at all. Now you have all this homework to do and not enough time to do it. The thing I do is this: As soon as I get home, I start on homework, then if I start to get

Q. My vacation activities are ruined by my selfish friend. We're on a trip with my family, and I'm always buying everything. She makes me buy her way into the pool and makes me pay for the movies we rent. Should I tell her how I feel . . . or should I just totally ditch her? What would you do?

—Karly, 13, Nebraska

1 I'd just come out and tell her that you aren't Miss Moneybags! She has to pay her own way.

Mostly disagree   Somewhat disagree   Somewhat agree   Mostly agree

2 Make sure there wasn't a misunderstanding when you started on the trip. Did she think your family was paying her way?

Mostly disagree   Somewhat disagree   Somewhat agree   Mostly agree

3 Just be kind, and the next time there is something to pay for, say, "Can you pay this time? We can take turns."

Mostly disagree   Somewhat disagree   Somewhat agree   Mostly agree

4 Tell your parents what is going on. Let them handle it.

Mostly disagree   Somewhat disagree   Somewhat agree   Mostly agree

5 Just suggest you do free things such as walk on the beach or visit a mall.

Mostly disagree   Somewhat disagree   Somewhat agree   Mostly agree

stressed, I take a 5-minute break and just relax and listen to my favorite singer or group. I don't go out with friends or anything because getting an education is a lot more important than friends. You can always go out with your friends on the weekend, but school is your future. Therefore, you should watch your grades and take it very seriously. Just remember, everything you need is right in your head—if you choose to use it! Good luck!

—Lindsey B., 14, Indiana

Put the problem into perspective: Is it really worth getting stressed over? Never forget to smile. By smiling, the muscles in and around your mouth change and send signals to your brain that calm you. Talk to your friends or family. Everyone has been through stress and would love to help you.

—Bree M., USA

Always eat a sensible meal. Get a good night's sleep also. Rest is very important.

—Tierney H., USA

What's the Best Way to Stop Being Too Emotional?

The Problem Dear Being Your Best: Sometimes I cry or yell at people, and I don't know why. I can get really sad or depressed for no reason. My parents say I'm moody because I want to be alone a lot. Everything that happens to me is a really big deal. Sometimes, out of nowhere, I get the giggles, and my friends think I'm nuts!

—Anonymous, USA

Be Happy

Draw a picture of the last time you made someone else really happy. What happened?

A Solution

You've probably heard it before, but when you are growing into a young woman, your shifting hormones are responsible for a huge part of how you feel. Sometimes you overreact when something bad happens. You have a lot of self-doubts. You worry about being an early bloomer or a late bloomer. Is there something wrong with you? Most likely, the answer is no.

Here are some ideas about how to get some control over your emotions.

1. Don't deny that your feelings exist. Don't "bottle up" your disappointments. If someone has hurt you, or if you've hurt them, don't pretend it's okay or didn't happen. On the other hand, if you are really hysterically happy and giggly about something great that's happened and it is annoying people, take a deep calming breath and celebrate with friends.

2. If you've already gotten your first period and you feel overly emotional, look at your calendar each month. If it's only a few days before your period, chances are that hormones are greatly responsible. Keep track in a notebook of how you feel during these times each month so that you can expect and plan for these feelings.

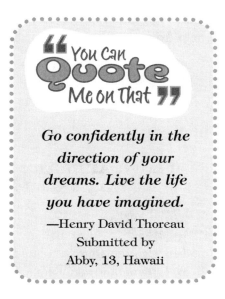

"You Can Quote Me On That"

Go confidently in the direction of your dreams. Live the life you have imagined.
—Henry David Thoreau
Submitted by
Abby, 13, Hawaii

3. Don't isolate yourself. If you find yourself moping around in your room, get out. Talk about your feelings with

friends, your older sister, or an adult you trust. "Did you ever feel like this?" is usually answered with "Sure!" Talk it out.

4. Join in a girl talk group with friends. If you don't want to talk to the girls in your area, get online each week on agirlsworld.com in the chat village. Check the chat calendar for Getting and Giving Advice sessions. This is your chance to talk about problems that are making you sad or mad or even about changes that you think are cool. Sharing makes life so much easier.

5. Strong feelings and worries about changes in your body or life are normal. But what if you really feel blue all the time? Or what if you find yourself purposely "acting up" and being loud or overly dramatic just to get attention? It's a good idea to go talk to a counselor at school or at church or talk to a doctor to make sure you're not suffering from depression. Don't be afraid to ask for help. You're worth it, girl!

—Written with advice from Lynn and Karen

I Love Animals! What's the Best Way I Can Help Them?

The Problem Dear Being Your Best: I care about animals and hate to see animals treated unkindly, but how can I really help? Do you know any animal sanctuaries in the London area where I could help?

—Alice, 13, England

A Solution Dear Alice: I'm glad to hear you care so much for animals! It is very sad to see animals treated unkindly; and sadly, it happens much too often. But there is plenty you can do to help! Check out some of my ideas, but make sure your 'rents agree before you go ahead!

Have a look in your local yellow pages or other phone book, or even phone to find out where your local animal sanctuaries or shelters are. You will have to phone the place up before you go, though, to make sure you don't have to be a certain age or need certain qualifications to help out. Most places will gladly welcome you!

Why not put an advertisement in the local post office to be a pet sitter, or a dog, cat, or bunny walker so that people who are going away don't have to leave their pets home alone, or so elderly people can have some help with exercising their pets properly!

Why not set up a club with some of your friends and give it a name so you can all watch out for mistreated animals, or maybe take animals that have been injured to your local vet or SPCA. Make sure you don't trespass on anyone's land or take away someone's pet by mistake! But do look out for hedgehogs (in the U.K. area), birds, badgers, cats, dogs, and other animals that have been injured on the road.

You Can Quote Me On That

Welcome anything that comes to you, but do not long for anything else.
—André Gide
Submitted by
Kara, 13, New Zealand

Be CAREFUL and maybe get an adult to help. You don't want to be knocked down, too. Also, injured animals in pain often bite, so wear gloves when trying to gently move them.

Why not make birdseed nets and feeders and string them up in your garden? Bird seed is inexpensive and easy to obtain, and birds always need lots of food when it is cold because

Talk About

Q. I want to be my best at dances, but I am really skittish when it comes to that kind of stuff. I just get really nervous and say what I don't mean to say, and afterwards I could kick myself. What should I do to have a better time and not look so awkward?

— Ashley, 13, USA

1 I'd go to the dance with a group of friends (all girls or girls and guys), then hang with the group. There's safety and fun in numbers.

Mostly disagree   Somewhat disagree   Somewhat agree   Mostly agree

2 If you go alone, whatever you do, don't just hang against the wall by yourself. That's where the nervous feelings start. Talk to other girls or guy friends who don't make you nervous.

Mostly disagree   Somewhat disagree   Somewhat agree   Mostly agree

3 Just keep your mouth shut. Smile and be friendly, but when you feel nervous, stop yourself from babbling and getting embarrassed.

Mostly disagree   Somewhat disagree   Somewhat agree   Mostly agree

4 Forget the girl-boy pressure and just dance in a big group with your gal pals. Most of the nerdy feelings come from waiting to be asked to dance.

Mostly disagree   Somewhat disagree   Somewhat agree   Mostly agree

5 As soon as you get there, go up to a guy and ask him to dance. If he says no, go to the next guy. This will be way better than just hanging back being nervous.

Mostly disagree   Somewhat disagree   Somewhat agree   Mostly agree

there is a shortage of good food.

Leave a small bowl of water and a small bowl of cat food outside your back door (or on the edge of your land) so hedgehogs, badgers, and other animals have something to eat. Don't put it too close to your house, though, as this will encourage them to come into your trash bins and practically destroy them!

I hope you like some of these ideas.

— Charlie, 13, England

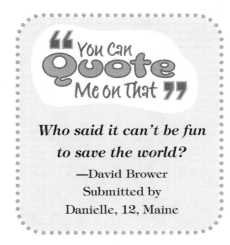

Who said it can't be fun to save the world?
—David Brower
Submitted by
Danielle, 12, Maine

Being Your Best at Whatever You Do

What's the Best Way to Start a Band?

The Problem Dear Being Your Best: I really want to start a band or singing group with a couple of my friends. The only problem is, I have no idea how to go about it! The biggest problem is, you need people who can play instruments if you want to start a band. The only instrument I or any of my friends can play is the piano!

—Samantha, 11, USA

A Solution Dear Samantha: Because none of you play any instruments, you have a couple of options. You could just be a singing group with prerecorded music, like the Backstreet Boys or Britney Spears. The only problem is, for now you can only sing other people's songs.

You Dream, Girl!

What do you dream about doing and being someday?

If you want to write and play your own music, you will need more of a complete band. To do this, you could advertise around your school or town for some people who can play the kind of instruments you want. This would be a good way to make some new friends, and maybe you'll even find a cute guy for the drums or something. Make sure these are people you could get along with so there aren't fights or anything. You don't want to have a split before things get started. Once you guys start practicing, you can think about performing in front of your school. Just try to have fun with it!

—Karla, 16, California

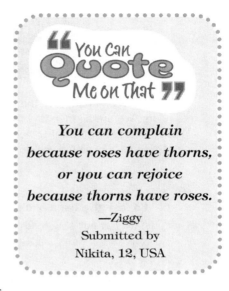

You can complain because roses have thorns, or you can rejoice because thorns have roses.
—Ziggy
Submitted by
Nikita, 12, USA

What's the Best Way to Get into a Chorus or Choir?

Thanks to Sheri from Oregon for telling us about the Portland Symphonic Girl choir. This incredible group of girls has 145 members that audition every year—even returning singers. Here's what their director looks for when evaluating a singer

Q. My friends and I have this band, and we have three lead singers. We are all friends, but one of our singers can't sing well at ALL. I don't want to hurt her feelings, but it's ruining our group. What would you do?

— Kim, 13, California

1 I'd just give her a back-up part that lets her participate but not sing lead.

Mostly disagree   Somewhat disagree   Somewhat agree   Mostly agree

2 Take her aside and tell her that she's a little off key and help her practice her part more.

Mostly disagree   Somewhat disagree   Somewhat agree   Mostly agree

3 Team up with the other girls and offer to help her improve her voice.

Mostly disagree   Somewhat disagree   Somewhat agree   Mostly agree

4 You'll just have to tell her that you love her, but she has to stay on key or leave the group.

Mostly disagree   Somewhat disagree   Somewhat agree   Mostly agree

5 I'd just record her singing her part alone, play it back, and let her hear for herself how bad she is. Maybe she'll improve or leave the group.

Mostly disagree   Somewhat disagree   Somewhat agree   Mostly agree

for membership in their group.

- How accurately can you sing your part?
- When other people are singing, can you hold your part and be steady and confident?
- Does your voice have a nice tone, and are you in tune?
- This group performs, so do you have a facial expression that is "alive!"?
- What's your attitude? You have to able to get along in a group. A positive attitude is necessary.
- Can you pay attention during rehearsals?
- Can you learn and memorize your music quickly?
- Do you have a good attendance record at rehearsals and performances?
- Do you listen to the director when he or she tries to guide you?
- When you say you will do something, will you do it? Are you responsible?

—Sheri, 14, Oregon

THE ART MILLENNIUM

There are so many different styles of art that it is hard to learn about them all unless you go to this site. Find artists, styles, and pictures.

www.art-encyclopedia.com/

MUSICALLY INCLINED

This site is for all you music lovers. It has everything from the music history to information about the musicians who wrote it.

library.thinkquest.org/C00146F/?tqskip=1

Q. I'm 11, in 6th grade, and love my doll, Kirsten! I'm NEVER getting rid of her or giving or throwing her away! But when do you think it's time to grow out of dolls? Is liking dolls weird?

— Bree, 11, Missouri

1 You can always like dolls. There are grown-ups who collect dolls. By 13, however, you should just put her away.

   Mostly disagree   Somewhat disagree   Somewhat agree   Mostly agree

2 Hey, you're only 11. When you are older, you'll just lose interest in playing with her, so don't worry.

   Mostly disagree   Somewhat disagree   Somewhat agree   Mostly agree

3 If your friends still play with dolls, don't worry about it.

   Mostly disagree   Somewhat disagree   Somewhat agree   Mostly agree

4 Get a cool display case for her, dress her in her best outfit, and just decorate with her.

   Mostly disagree   Somewhat disagree   Somewhat agree   Mostly agree

5 There is no set age to stop playing with dolls. If your friends think it's weird, just play with her in private.

   Mostly disagree   Somewhat disagree   Somewhat agree   Mostly agree

Being Your Best at Whatever You Do **193**

Journalize It!

Doodle

Draw a picture of the way you are now.

Draw a picture of yourself in twenty years. What will you be doing?

Q. I really want to be a country singer, and I think I am good enough and would really like to start off young like Billy Gilman, Aaron Carter, Sammie, etc. But I really don't know were to start. What would you do?

—Courtney, 12, Washington

1 Get your parents on your side. Ask them to help you reach your dream.

Mostly disagree Somewhat disagree Somewhat agree Mostly agree

2 You should take singing lessons and start singing at church, school, anywhere you can find an audience.

Mostly disagree Somewhat disagree Somewhat agree Mostly agree

3 Practice, then make a sample tape and send it to local radio stations.

Mostly disagree Somewhat disagree Somewhat agree Mostly agree

4 Practice, make a demo tape or CD, then find out who the managers of your favorite singers are and send the tape to them.

Mostly disagree Somewhat disagree Somewhat agree Mostly agree

5 School has to come first. Just develop your singing on the side.

Mostly disagree Somewhat disagree Somewhat agree Mostly agree

What's the Best Way to Make a Student Video?

Lights, Camera, Action! Recently, my French II class at school had the privilege of making student French videos. It was a lot of hard work, but it was fun, too. Our class divided up into groups of five students and got to work. My group consisted of four of my friends and me. We thought it would be simple: Write the play, film it, turn it in, and get a grade. It did seem simple, but it took a little more effort than that.

First, we had to write the play. Simple as that may sound, we had a few obstacles to overcome. For one thing, it had to be in French, so that limited our creativity. Plus, we aren't professional camera people or directors, so we had to think of something simple yet entertaining. We only had six school days to work on it, and then it wasn't all day. It was only one hour a day while we were in French class.

A GIRL LIKE YOU

Step out on your quest for success by taking a look at your roots. Be proud of your family history. Find out how your look back at the past can help your future.

www.agirllikeu.com/quest_looking.asp

To change and to change for the better are two different things.

—German Proverb
Submitted by
Xena, 12, Texas

Unfortunately, our whole group was in band, and this assignment was right in the middle of the busiest part of the season. It took our lunch periods for the whole week, and we worked right up until 9:00 the night before it was due, typing it up and proofreading it again and again. But we got it in and made a 95/A!

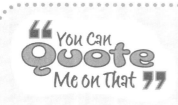

Look at everything as though you were seeing it for the first time or the last time. Then your time on earth will be filled with glory.
—Betty Smith
Submitted by
Jena, 14, California

Next was filming. This was the hard part. Our play took place completely outside, so bad weather, along with conflicting schedules, put off filming until the Thursday, Friday, and Monday before it was due. Nothing like waiting till the last minute, huh! But even before filming could begin, we needed credits for the beginning, a narrator, a camera and tripod, and, of course, parental supervision. Once all of these things were gathered and the scenes were set up, filming began. We first practiced the lines and the movement needed. We used two tapes so we could see where we needed to stand and how loud to speak.

We called our practice tape our "Blooper Tape," and we looked at it after every scene. The lighting caught us off guard, too. If one scene was in the daylight and we were filming after school, we had to rehearse and film before the sun went down. Our film was only 5 minutes long, and it took two days to film. Now I know why a 3-hour movie takes two years to film!

But in the end, we turned it in on time and ended up getting a perfect-plus 310 out of 300 on it! We were so excited that our hard work had paid off. In case any of you out there are planning on making a video in the near future, whether for school or just for the heck of it, here are a few tips to help your movie really get off the ground and impress your family and friends!

Tips for Making a Film

1. Put a lot of thought into your script; don't over-shoot your abilities. Your play will look better if it is simple than if it is too hard and looks fake.

2. Give yourself plenty of time. I know it seems as though we waited till the last minute on everything, but it really stressed us out. Filming is more fun if everything goes smoothly.

3. Learn how to use your camera. Have your parents teach you how to work the

JASON XII 2001: A LIVING LABORATORY

If you're interested in Hawaiian volcanoes, coral, culture, and more, then this a place for you. You can meet the team and find out what Jason XII is all about.

www.jasonproject.org /expeditions/jason12/

The grand essentials to happiness in this life are something to do, something to love, and something to hope for.

—Joseph Addison
Submitted by
Megan, 16, Texas

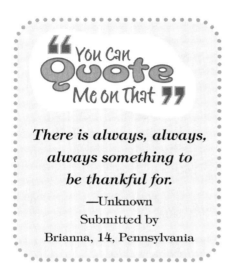

There is always, always, always something to be thankful for.
—Unknown
Submitted by
Brianna, 14, Pennsylvania

camera. If it has a "fade" ability, then learn it and use it. It adds a real professional look. (P.S. Don't forget to take off the date and time clock!)

4. Use a tripod. You are more likely to get good feedback if watching your video doesn't give people a headache. Not everyone can handle that *Blair Witch Project*–type filming.

5. Watch your lighting. Be sure you'll be able to see the actors and actresses when you watch the tape. You don't want it too dark or too bright.

6. Use two tapes. If you do this, then you can see how you look before you film it for real. Plus, if you mess up, you can put them behind your finished video as funny bloopers. Hey, didn't you like the bloopers on *A Bug's Life?*

Well, that's about everything. Oh, most important, have fun! Be creative. So get out there and start filming.
Lights, Camera, Action!

—Lindsay, 15, Louisiana

Join the Fun!

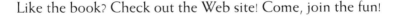

Like the book? Check out the Web site! Come, join the fun!

What People Are Saying About Us

USA TODAY: **Featured as "Everything a Girl Could Want"**:
"Since 1996, the only free online magazine with daily, weekly, and monthly features written and edited by girls and teens."

Snipped from *The New York Times:*
"There are a few wonderful sites that present utterly absorbing, enjoyable and comparatively safe places for pre-teenage and teen-age girls. In fact, I'm convinced that, taken together, Web sites like the ones reviewed here—Girl Tech, Purple Moon, and A Girl's World— may just be the 'killer app' for girls. . . . A Girl's World is run by a staff of volunteers, almost all of whom are girls

themselves. The result is an admirable, if unsophisticated, e-zine for girls (that is an) amazing testament to the creative energy of its visitors. . . . Although the presentation of A Girl's World is simple and straightforward—nearly everything is rendered in text—it has a greater abundance of spirit than a Girl Scout cookout . . . refreshing."

Snipped from Spun Gold Award for Excellence from Kid's Domain:
"This is a wonderful site for girls, with great content. Any girl who wants to can submit an article and get credit for it! They will also receive a free year's membership to Gold Key Circle and the safety measures (in a Gold Key) are exemplary. There is no advertising, no hidden agenda, just girls having fun!

"I simply can't praise this site enough! I couldn't find one thing I didn't like about it, and I am pretty picky about what I let my girls do and see. I have never been crazy about the idea of kids chat rooms, either, but I like the idea of the membership, password-protected chat rooms. . . . The articles are well written and informative, the crafts are fun, the teen advice column is right on target with teen concerns, and being able to contribute your own articles is a wonderful idea! A Girl's World Online Club is definitely deserving of our Gold Award for Excellence."

Snipped from the *Los Angeles Times*, reviewed by www.4kids.org:
"A Girl's World Online Clubhouse is an incredible online experience just for girls. As 'the space where girls rule the place,' this monthly magazine is for girls of the 90s. There is so much you could do, you could stay for days. Make new friends, get to know women with dynamite

careers, find directions for neat stuff you can make, and lots more! Girls are in the clubhouse, waiting for you to come share your thoughts on a million different subjects. So go, girl, and have a blast at the place 'where it's cool to be a girl!'"

What Girls Say About AGW

"This place rules!! I spend like 20 hours on here a month!"
— Jen

"I think it's awesome that people like you guys could start something like this. It's cool, and safe, just what online girlz need. KEEP UP THE GOOD WORK!"
— Shelley

"The Penpal program is great! And I LOVE the Babysitting classes! That's why its a big thing 4 me. (The teacher's) doing a GREAT job! GIRLSWORLD RULES!! Love,"
— Melissa

"I think the club is great. I pop in to the page every day when I get time."
— Aviva

"I got to talk to a real rocket scientist! I can't wait to tell all my friends. I love science. I want to be a scientist when I grow up."
— Holly

"This is one cool place for GIRLS where girls aren't expected to be wimps."
— Mallory

"When I first got here, I thought this would be all about makeup, prissy stuff like that. But it's not, so it's cool!"
—Samantha

"Hey! I just wanted to thank you for making this so fun. I am 15, and I am having lots of fun and was surprised to find people my age when I found this site. *THANKS ALOT!*"
—R DUDA

What Adults Say About AGW

"I recently had the pleasure of visiting AGW and was thrilled with what I found! It's such a pleasure to see a magazine for girls that doesn't dwell on 'hot hunks' or how to increase your (physical) appeal. Girls of this age desperately need to be valued for who they are, not for how close they come to some Hollywood ideal . . . it's wonderful that you profile women of true achievement, not just models and actresses. Young girls need to have women to look up to, and you are doing a great job in providing role models."
—Kelly

"I very much believe in what you're doing for young girls. I think it's critical to have girl sites that don't just hawk the latest makeup trends, but that really promote independence and unique thinking. In any case, kudos to you for what you're doing. We need more young girls to have self-confidence."
—Heather I.

Awards

New members join every day, based on the recommendations of teachers, parents, and major search engines like Yahooligans, which rated us one of the "coolest" magazines on the Web for girls.

AGW was the first online site for girls recommended by CNN Interactive. Our Penpal Spectacular was cited by a major consumer reporting magazine. We've been awarded The Point's coveted "Top 5% of the Web" award and were cited as the best site on the Web for girls by the *San Diego Union Tribune*. We've been featured in other media, such as the *Los Angeles Times'* Cutting Edge, on KFI 640 AM radio, and by *Family PC* magazine, along with numerous other awards.

We are recommended and listed by Sprint, Lycos, CNN, Prodigy Kids Pages, Cochran Kids Sites, Kidscom, About Me, 4Kids.org, Peekaboo, World Village, WWWomen.com, On Ramp-Canada, Femina, and Whidbey-Australia. Altogether about 3,000 other sites have created links to A Girl's World Online Clubhouse.

Use the Gold Key Chat Club to Meet New Friends!

Give and get advice, get a penpal without publishing your e-mail address, and do what you love to do—chat, meet great guests, post on message boards, play games, get access to our online Babysitter's Certificate class—all for free! (Our Babysitter's Certificate is available for an extra charge once you pass the test.) It's a cool deal, a whole year of fun! That's a $15.00 value—FREE for any girl who buys this book! Fill out this form to join the club!

What Gold Key Is: Gold Key is a private, member-supported chat club just for girls and teens the world over, ages 7 to 17. For information about what this members-only chat club is all about, go here:

www.agirlsworld.com/clubgirl/gold-key/chatworks.html

Privacy and Information Use Policy: A Girl's World Online Clubhouse does not rent, sell, or give out e-mail addresses, addresses, mailing lists, or personally identifiable information about girls to anyone else. Ever. Period. All information on this form is kept strictly private and is used solely for signup, security, and contact information. We will not provide this information to any third party.

This signed permission form will complete your daughter's application. We will create a Gold Key Chat Club user name for her and mark her account as "paid" with full access for one year just as soon as this signed permission form is received. Thank you for helping us provide a safe, fun chat area for girls on the Web!

Problems? Get Help!

It can take up to a week after we receive your signed permission form to give your daughter access to the chat club. If you don't hear from us within ten days, please do the following: Send a message to lost-gk-password@agirlsworld.com. The computer will let you know if we have a Gold Key user name for your daughter. If you get back an e-mail that says "no user name" and you sent in your form, please send an e-mail describing the problem to gk-problems@agirlsworld.com, and we will check it out.

Thanks again to Prima Publishing and their support in making this the place where girls and teens rule the Web!

A Girl's World Gold Key Circle Chat Club Membership Form

I, (Parent's Name) _____ certify that I am the parent or legal guardian of (Daughter's Name) _____, age _____.

I hereby give my permission for my daughter to participate in the Gold Key Circle Chat Club. By signing up for and using this chat service, my daughter and I agree that we have read and agreed to follow these chat club rules at http://www.agirlsworld.com/clubgirl/gold-key/rules.html and Terms of Service at http://www.agirlsworld.com/clubgirl/gold-key/terms.html. I understand that AGW reserves the right to delete without warning or refund any member of the Gold Key Circle Chat Club who violates the Chat Club rules or Terms of Service.

Signed:

(Parent's Signature) _____ Date _____

Passcode Contact Information: We'll send your daughter's Gold Key passcode by e-mail to the e-mail address below.

E-mail address _____

If we're unable to complete your daughter's chat club signup, our club will send a postcard to your mailing address. We will not provide this information to any third party.

Mailing address:

Street:_____ Apt./PO:_____

City: _____ State: _____ Zip Code: _____

Country: (if not USA) _____

International Postal Code: _____

Finish Your Signup

- Parents, please tear out, fill out, and sign this form. No facsimiles, please.
- Don't forget to check to see that the e-mail address is filled out so we can complete your signup.
- Mail your completed form to:

A Girl's World Online Clubhouse
Attn: Prima Books: Free Chatclub/Penpals Offer
825 College Blvd. PBO 102-442
Oceanside, CA 92057

Meet the Editor

PHOTO BY CANDICE CLEARY

My name is Sara Sauceda, and I am 15 years old. I was born on September 11, 1985, in San Diego, California. I currently live with my parents, two dogs, and a rabbit, but I also have an older brother and sister. I think I am a rather outgoing person and very cheerful.

I enjoy hanging out with my friends, riding horses, and playing soccer. I also love spending time with my family. The most challenging thing I have ever accomplished is staying on task. There are so many distractions these days, and I am proud to say that I have overcome them so far. I have been a member (on and off) of A Girls World since 1996. My favorite thing about these books is that they are helping girls all over the world, and I am very proud to be a part of it all. My advice to other girls who want to be writers is to write what you know and go from there. My dream for the future is to attend the University of California, San Diego, and hopefully become a microbiologist. The thing I enjoy the most about being a girl today is I have the equal amount of rights and respect as a male.

Meet the Editor

If you have any questions or comments about this book, e-mail me by visiting www.agirlsworld.com. I'd really love hearing from you. My penpal number is 210893. I hope you enjoy *Talking About Being Your Best* as much as I enjoyed editing it.